THE GREAT
MEMORIAL DAY
FIRE OF 1945
AND OTHER
SCHUYLKILL COUNTY
DISASTERS

MICHAEL R. GLORE AND MICHAEL J. KITSOCK

THE
History
PRESS

Published by The History Press
Charleston, SC
www.historypress.com

First published 2025

Manufactured in the United States

ISBN 9781467158831

Library of Congress Control Number: 2024950741

Notice: The information in this book is true and complete to the best of our knowledge. It is offered without guarantee on the part of the authors or The History Press. The authors and The History Press disclaim all liability in connection with the use of this book.

To the Fallen Firefighters

CONTENTS

CONTENTS

1

DIVINITY AND JUSTICE

JUNE 15, 1926

The Prohibition years soon fostered a burgeoning business in illegal booze, gambling and prostitution throughout Schuylkill County, Pennsylvania. Roadhouses were established by criminal elements where such activities occurred "around the clock." With thousands of miners as potential "patrons," the roadhouses flourished. The small mining community of Mahanoy Plane, a village of over 1,500 residents in the 1920s, had several such establishments, the most famous being the Tilly Billy Café and Hotel on the High Road. Incensed by these immoral activities in his town, the Reverend Patrick J. Fleming, pastor of the Holy Rosary Roman Catholic Church, soon waged a crusade from his pulpit to cleanse this Christian community of such vices. Public indignation soon grew, and a meeting of concerned townspeople was held in front of the Tilly Billy on the evening of June 14, 1926. Several hundred people heard stirring addresses against the establishment, and public opinion was soon crystalizing against its proprietor, Frank Fotte of Shenandoah.

THE PLOT

Antagonized and enraged by the repeated sermons of the good vicar and prominent townspeople against his business establishment, Frank Fotte and several of his Tilly Billy cohorts soon plotted revenge against the leader of this campaign, the Reverend Patrick J. Fleming. How dare this pious man campaign against his business? Who was this man of the cloth to judge moral and immoral activities? What if more residents of the town or the employees of the nearby Mahanoy Plane itself, Reading Railroad repair shops, East and West Bear Ridge Collieries all turned against them and this thriving business? Something needed to be done and done right away. Fotte was heard to say by several of his patrons, "We will fix him!" The conspirators plotted to burn Father Fleming alive while he was sleeping in his own rectory, thus ending his "noble" campaign and showing everyone in the area who really wielded the greater power and the greater control in this coal town.

FIRE! FIRE! FIRE!!!

In the early morning hours of June 15, 1926, following a steady rainstorm, three cars sped along West Main Street in Mahanoy Plane and stopped in front of the Holy Rosary Rectory. In the cars were Frank Fotte, Carlo Romalo, Tony Scatton and Tony Spallone. William McCarthy lived opposite the church on the High Road. As a light sleeper, McCarthy, a member of the Holy Rosary Church, heard the approach of the cars. Peering out his bedroom window, he witnessed the strange appearance of the stopped vehicles at the rectory about 2:00 a.m. McCarthy watched as several men emerged, walked around the rectory, returned to their vehicles and departed. About fifteen minutes later, according to McCarthy, the cars reappeared and again stopped at the rectory. The car engines were turned off, seemingly to eliminate extra noise, and several men emerged once again, carrying containers. Returning to their cars, one man hurled a burning ball of cotton waste onto the rectory porch, and a tremendous explosion ensued. William McCarthy could not believe what he had just seen, and now before his very eyes, the beautiful three-story frame Victorian rectory was a massive ball of fire.

In a hasty attempt to depart the crime scene, one of the drivers flooded the engine of his Peerless getaway car and the vehicle refused to start. After repeated attempts at starting the engine failed, the driver quickly tried unsuccessfully to remove the license plate from the back of the vehicle. Failing again, he soon ran into the cover of darkness as McCarthy and other town residents, awakened by the explosion, rapidly converged on the burning rectory. The stalled car was abandoned at the scene and later provided sufficient evidence to the police that this indeed was a despicable and irrefutable incendiary act perpetrated against the good priest Patrick J. Fleming.

The gutted front of the once-handsome rectory of the Holy Rosary Roman Catholic Church, which was firebombed on June 15, 1926, in Mahanoy Plane. One can only imagine the terror the large frame building's occupants experienced as they attempted to escape the flames. *Kitsock collection.*

NARROW ESCAPE

Abruptly awakened by the explosion, Lillian Fleming, sister of the reverend, and Annie Martin, aged housekeeper, alerted the good pastor and attempted an escape out the front stairwell. Intense heat and severe smoke soon drove them back several times. Another escape attempt was made through a back stairwell, where heat and smoke were less severe. Reverend Fleming soon followed his sister and housekeeper to safety through this exit, escaping only with their nightclothes. All possessions and furnishings were consumed by the flames. Those village residents not awakened by the explosion were soon alerted of the disaster by the sounding of the town's fire whistle. Members of the American Hose Company No. 2 of Mahanoy Plane rushed to the firehouse and immediately pulled the town's hose cart, its only means of fire protection, to the scene. With quick action the Mahanoy Plane firefighters, realizing that the rectory was already lost, placed several hose lines onto the nearby church, attempting to prevent the flames from gaining added headway and possibly destroying the church and the entire block. With the church's destruction threatened, Reverend Doolin, visiting family members in Mahanoy Plane, rushed into the church and removed the most blessed sacrament to a place of safety.

A BATTLE ENSUES

As the flames soon grew into an inferno, additional help from nearby communities was immediately summoned by telephone. Shenandoah Borough Police, on receiving the call for help, quickly struck Box 26, Main and Center Streets, to summon their fire department. Shenandoah Fire Chief Dill Jones then dispatched the Columbia Hose Company No. 1 with their 1921 American La France and the Phoenix Fire Company No. 2 with their 1923 American La France to Mahanoy Plane. On learning of the severity of the fire now threatening the church, many members of the Shenandoah Fire Department responded to the scene in their cars to lend assistance.

Next to arrive on location was the Continental Hose Company No. 3 of Gilberton in their 1924 International pumper. The "Ducktowners," as they were known, working with the Shenandoah fire lads, soon placed additional hose lines on the rectory fire itself. The Ducktowners were

The heavily damaged rear portion of the Holy Rosary rectory is evidenced in the photo, as is the close proximity of the church itself. The effective work of firefighters that morning saved the church and surrounding properties. *Kitsock collection.*

followed by the Rangers Hose Company of Girardville, Good Will Fire Company No. 1 of Frackville and the Humane Fire Company No. 1 of Mahanoy City. Following a three-hour battle, firefighters were able to douse the flames, thus saving the church and adjoining row homes from impending disaster. All that remained was a blackened shell of the three-story rectory, a stark reminder of the lawlessness and defiance prevalent at that time in Schuylkill County.

JUSTICE PREVAILS

As soon as the remaining embers were extinguished, local and state police were summoned to the scene. The Peerless "getaway" car abandoned at the fire was carefully removed to Flynn's Garage in Mahanoy Plane for safekeeping. A close examination of the car revealed several clues: business cards advertising Frank Fotte's Restaurant in Shenandoah; a bill from Thomas Bevan, a plumber from Mahanoy Plane, for work performed at the Tilly Billy Hotel; a blackjack; a revolver; and a box of cartridges.

Out of the ashes of the Holy Rosary rectory fire came a call for better fire protection for the village of Mahanoy Plane. Francis "Skip" Kelly and Gerald McCabe Sr. (*standing*) of the American Hose Company No. 2 of Mahanoy Plane pose proudly with the company's 1927 American LaFrance pumper, which was purchased following the rectory fire. *Kitsock collection.*

Dr. L.F. Donaghue of Mahanoy Plane visited Police Chief Daniel T. McKelvey of Hazleton and engaged him to bring the criminals to justice. So effective was Chief McKelvey's work that his own home was dynamited and left in ruins. Additionally, Detective Louis D. Buono of Schuylkill County and his assistant, Frank Post, performed excellent work on the case. It was Buono, who, after a long chase covering nearly all the large cities of the East, located Romalo in Baltimore and brought him back to Schuylkill County to serve a long prison term. All four perpetrators— Fotte, Romalo, Scatton and Spallone—were convicted of the crime in the Schuylkill County Court and sentenced to eight to sixteen years in the Schuylkill County Prison. The good residents of Schuylkill County soon rallied to the efforts of Reverend Fleming and began to rid the county of criminal roadhouses and brothels. Following the disastrous blaze, a fundraising effort commenced in Mahanoy Plane to purchase a new, motorized fire truck for the community. The American Hose Company No. 2 of Mahanoy Plane received a new American LaFrance fire truck on August 25, 1927, its first motorized vehicle. Thus ended a dark chapter in the Prohibition years of Schuylkill County, Pennsylvania.

2

A NIGHT TO REMEMBER

CANTWELL FIRE—JANUARY 22, 1947

Joseph McDonald feared the worst. On departing the Cantwell Hotel & Tavern on East Main Street in Girardville in the early morning hours of a bitterly cold January 22, 1947, he smelled smoke. Unable to locate the source of the odor, McDonald crossed Main Street just as flames erupted through the roof of the Anna Grumm house at 130 East Main Street. A house fire was now raging in the borough, and weather conditions could not be much worse—temperatures at or below zero with a fierce north wind howling. For Girardville residents, it would soon become a night to remember.

Summoning aid from other late-night patrons at Cantwell's, McDonald broke open the door to the Grumm house to arouse the sleeping family while his companions alerted neighboring residents of the danger. Another patron reported the fire to authorities. Soon the sounding of the Girardville Municipal Fire Alarm alerted both residents and volunteer firefighters from the town's two fire companies, the Girard Hose Company No. 1, situated nearby at 120–22 East Main Street, and the Rangers' Hose Company, located a few blocks away on West Ogden Street. Fed by a steady and brutally cold wind, the fire was spreading rapidly both east and west along Main Street. Arriving firefighters soon realized they had the battle of their lives on their hands against the fiery foe.

Fighting fires during bitter winter conditions can seriously test the mettle of even the most seasoned firefighters. Frozen hydrants, bone-chilling cold, razor-sharp winds, frostbite and icy conditions everywhere

Hampered by insufficient water pressure in the early stages of the fire, firefighters awaited help from neighboring communities to augment the water supply. The rapidly spreading flames—fanned by gale-force winds—continued to consume the properties along East Main Street in Girardville in 1947. *Girardville Historical Society*.

make life truly miserable for firefighters. Such were the conditions facing Girardville's volunteers as they raced to the scene of the blaze. Girard Hose Company members faced an even greater peril—their fire station was already threatened by the racing flames. Several businesses along East Main were also in danger, including Portz Shoe Store, Davies' Barber Shop, several apartments and the Cantwell Hotel & Tavern. With the absence of Girardville Fire Chief Thomas J. Kelly due to illness, Assistant Fire Chief Herbert Portz of the Girard Hose Company took command and began organizing firefighting efforts.

Within minutes, flames spread eastward and soon consumed the homes of Patrick McLaughlin and James Flynn. Spreading westward as well, the blaze now threatened Harold Davies's barbershop as well as the homes of Al Miller and Herbert Pryce. Girard Hose Company firefighters successfully removed their two Hahn pumpers and the community ambulance from their fire station as the flames spread ever closer to their building. The Rangers Hose Company soon arrived with their 1937 Hahn pumper, and both fire companies attempted to fight

With every crack and crash of the roofs and floors, embers shot skyward. At its height, the fire on East Main Street in Girardville spread rapidly through the buildings, with most in varying stages of collapse. *Girardville Historical Society*.

the developing inferno. Firefighting efforts, however, were thwarted by both low water pressure and frozen fire hydrants. Realizing the severity of the situation, Assistant Chief Portz made a frantic plea for help from neighboring communities.

First of the out-of-town companies to arrive was the American Hose Company No. 1 of Ashland in their 1942 Seagrave pumper, led by Ashland Fire Chief John Snyder. Snyder soon aided Assistant Chief Portz in organizing the firefighting tactics as the blaze, fed by gale-force winds, now developed into a conflagration and continued its assault on East Main Street businesses and residences. Next to arrive was the American Hose Company No. 2 of Mahanoy Plane in their 1927 American La France pumper. Seeing the futility of "hooking up" to a frozen fire hydrant, Mahanoy Plane firefighters drove their pumper several blocks to the Mahanoy Creek. With the assistance of neighbors, planks were laid into the creek bed and the truck was driven in. Soon the venerable "Alf" pumper was drafting water from the creek, and several excellent hose lines were established.

Above: A young lady glances backward as she and other citizens look over the destruction wrought by the flames along East Main Street in 1947. Structural steel framing is all that is identifiable with the building in the foreground. *Girardville Historical Society*.

Opposite, top: A lone, unmanned two-and-a-half-inch hose stream continues to pour water onto the ruins of the properties along East Main Street, creating strangely captivating ice sculptures. *Girardville Historical Society.*

Opposite, bottom: Battling in brutally cold conditions, firemen from Girardville and surrounding communities prevented the flames from extending to the adjacent wood frame properties along East Main Street. Note the wooden "Bangor Ladder" placed to the roof of an exposure building with the familiar tormentor poles placed on the sidewalk. *Girardville Historical Society*.

Arriving next were Gilberton's Continental Hose Company No. 3 with their 1942 Diamond-T/Oren pumper and manpower followed by the West End and Citizens' Fire Companies of the nearby village of Lost Creek, with their 1937 Hahn and 1942 Mack pumpers. The Good Will Hose Company No. 1 of Frackville rushed to the scene with its new 1947 Seagrave truck. Shenandoah sent two companies to the fire scene, the Phoenix and the Polish American companies, both arriving with their 1941 Mack pumpers. Last to arrive on scene was the West End Fire Company No. 5 of Mahanoy City with its 1929 Buffalo pumper.

As the severity of the situation became evident, neighbors and residents pitched in in the dual attempts to help the victims and stop the spread of the fire. Boiling pots of water provided by this helpful squad soon thawed several of the frozen hydrants enough for firefighters to establish some hose lines. Rather than watch their fellow neighbors lose all their possessions to the raging flames, teams of spirited citizens soon worked feverishly to save the furniture and valuable possessions of those threatened, carrying items across East Main Street to a position of safety. Hot coffee provided by neighbors helped thaw the frozen firefighters, enabling them to continue their now heroic efforts. Yet the fire continued its westward assault, spreading to and consuming the Girard Hose Company and Cantwell Hotel & Tavern. Portz Shoe Store, owned by Assistant Chief Raymond Portz, Davies' Barber Shop and several apartment buildings and homes now lay in ruins.

After a bitter, long, six-hour battle, weary firefighters finally brought the blaze under control. In the early morning light, the devastation along East Main Street became evident: eleven properties were destroyed, leaving thirty-six people homeless. The fire had consumed a half-block area in the heart of Girardville, an area of East Main Street bounded by Second, Vine and Oak Streets. Miraculously, only one injury was recorded: Harry Longlantz, a Girardville firefighter, who was overcome by smoke and hospitalized at the Miners' Hospital in Ashland. Property damage exceeded $250,000, and with such large-scale destruction, no cause for the fire was ever determined.

3

GONE WITH THE WIND

DECEMBER 15, 1949

Michael "Mickey" Bellekonich, aged seventeen of New Philadelphia, was proud of his after-school job. Mickey's responsibility was taking care of the coal-fired furnace in the boiler room of New Philadelphia's only movie theater, the Lyric. Just the previous night, Thursday, December 15, 1949, the Lyric boasted a packed house for the premiere showing of *Gone with the Wind*, starring Vivien Leigh and Clark Gable. Keeping the theater warm for the Friday evening showing, with another large crowd expected, would be his duty. The time was 3:00 p.m.

As Mickey opened the door to the boiler room of the theater, he was met by a large plume of heavy, black, acrid smoke. With the doorway open, the boiler room fire quickly gained intensity and began spreading rapidly. Racing to the Good Intent Fire Company, only a block away from the theater, Mickey sounded the town's fire alarm, summoning fire company volunteers and their U.S. Fire Apparatus pumper to the scene. A frantic call was also made to the nearby village of Cumbola. The Good Will Fire Company volunteer firefighters quickly responded in their new Ahrens-Fox pumper.

With two fire companies on scene, firefighters made a vain attempt to douse the flames using New Philadelphia's fire hydrant system. Two fire hydrants closest to the fire were opened, but firefighters' hopes of stopping this blaze were dashed. Virtually no water was available from the hydrant system. Blythe Township Water Authority officials later blamed the long-term drought as the culprit, with the reservoir supplying the borough of New

Philadelphia virtually depleted. Blythe Township water officials frantically tried to divert water from alternate sources into the New Philadelphia system. With no water available through the borough's hydrant system, the fire quickly developed into a raging inferno.

Built in 1921, at a time when movie theaters were gaining popularity, the Lyric boasted a seating capacity of six hundred, and it soon became a popular entertainment venue for the Schuylkill Valley. Located on Valley Street along Route 209, the theater stood as a landmark building in the center of the community. Owned by Mark Rubinsky, who once hailed from Shenandoah in northern Schuylkill County, the Lyric was managed by Mark's brother, Charles Rubinsky. Mark Rubinsky owned a chain of theaters in the region. The Lyric fire was the Rubinskys' first experience with a theater fire.

As flames raged into a conflagration, now threatening nearby homes, additional aid was summoned from the boroughs of Port Carbon and Palo Alto, several miles to the west, and the city of Pottsville. The Good Will Fire Company of Port Carbon responded in its Peter Pirsch pumper while the Citizens' Fire Company of Palo Alto sent its Seagrave pumper to the scene. Fire Chief George Smith of Pottsville dispatched the American Hose Company and its new American La France pumper. With the arrival of several additional pumpers and more manpower, water was drafted from the nearby Schuylkill River and relayed to the fire scene. By 4:30 p.m., however, the roof of the theater had collapsed, and the blaze now threatened the eight row homes adjoining the rear of the theater. Residents and neighbors in panic and fearing the worst soon removed furniture and possessions, many of which were thrown from second-story windows. With the timely arrival of water from the river, several two-and-a-half-inch hose lines were strategically placed into service, thus diminishing the threat of destruction to the nearby row homes.

News of the disastrous fire soon spread, and several hundred spectators converged on the site. Pennsylvania State Police as well as Port Carbon Fire Police managed to control the crowd at the scene. Soon other dangers also became apparent: high-voltage power lines severed by the flames dropped onto the nearby Reading Railroad tracks, thus electrifying the tracks and raising the peril of electrocution until Pennsylvania Power & Light workers cut the power to the area. Likewise, flaming embers were carried onto nearby roofs by air currents. Residents climbed onto their roofs with brooms and buckets of water to extinguish the embers. Finally, by 6:30 p.m., the fire had been declared under control.

Firemen desperately wait for water as flames roar from the Lyric Theater in New Philadelphia. Note the hose line stretched over the porch roof of the property to the right as well as the utility wires burning in front of the theater. *Schuylkill County Historical Society.*

New Philadelphia firefighters remained on the fire scene throughout the night, pouring water onto the charred remains and twisted girders of the once beautiful theater. Since the Lyric was only partially insured against fire, owner Mark Rubinsky decided not to rebuild a theater on this site. Perhaps the growing popularity of a new venue of entertainment— television—cemented his decision. In a tragic twist of fate, *Gone with the Wind*, ironically was the last movie ever shown at New Philadelphia's Lyric Theater.

4

"MY GOD, GET ME THE FIRE DEPARTMENT!"

SEPTEMBER 20, 1949

Reading Railroad's early morning passenger train, Train No. 91, departed Philadelphia promptly at seven o'clock on its daily northbound route to Shamokin in the Pennsylvania anthracite coal region. On this day, Tuesday, September 20, 1949, Engineer Charles Moyer of Philadelphia was at the throttle of steam-powered Reading locomotive No. 216. While generally light with passengers, Train No. 91 served primarily as the "Mailman" for numerous cities and towns along the way, delivering sorted mail to these communities, including my (Michael Kitsock) own hometown, Mahanoy Plane. Train No. 91 departing on this day was no exception, as it exited the famous Reading Company trainshed in downtown Philadelphia on time with only two passenger coaches and four baggage/mail cars. In addition to Engineer Moyer, trainmen working Train No. 91 that day were William Gift, John Marszake and James Seitzinger of Philadelphia; Kenneth Beck and John Aulenbach of Schuylkill Haven; and Elmer Hottenstein of Laureldale.

Losing most of its passenger load in the cities of Reading and Pottsville, Train No. 91 departed the Pottsville station at 10:10 a.m., heading east to its next sizeable community, Tamaqua. Tragedy, however, soon struck. At a minor grade crossing at Newbold Street in nearby Port Carbon, two miles east of the Pottsville station, a tractor trailer driven by thirty-three-year-old Clarence Goetz of Gap, Lancaster County, and owned by Matlack Inc. of Philadelphia, carrying 4,500 gallons of highly volatile gasoline, entered the railroad crossing moments before the train arrived. At 10:18 a.m., a collision occurred between the steam locomotive of the train and the gasoline tanker.

Throngs of spectators were drawn to the horrific scene in Port Carbon as the damaged baggage and mail cars of Train No. 91 are clearly visible, as is the cab of the tractor-trailer involved in the horrific accident. *Schuylkill County Historical Society.*

According to the Interstate Commerce Commission (ICC) report, estimated train speed at the time of the accident was twenty-nine miles per hour; the truck's speed was estimated at four miles per hour. A massive explosion immediately erupted from the ruptured gasoline tank, spewing flaming gasoline into several directions and setting ablaze two of the baggage/mail cars of the train. Burning gasoline soon flowed into Port Carbon's sewers and storm drains, setting ablaze everything in its path, including two nearby homes, an automobile and a garage.

Startled by the severity of the explosion and viewing pitch-black columns of smoke arising from the scene, citizens and firefighters rushed forth to the area. A local neighbor and witness, Mrs. G. Paul Starr, shouted to a telephone operator, "My God, get me the fire department!" Soon the sounding of the town fire alarm summoned volunteers of the Good Will Fire Company of Port Carbon to the scene. Arriving in their Peter Pirsch pumper, Port Carbon firefighters were confronted by a dreadful sight: a blazing inferno at the Newbold Street collision site and two nearby homes, a garage and an automobile already on fire from the burning gasoline. Moreover, three railroad employees were trapped in a burning baggage/ mail car. Unknown to the firefighters, however, would be how many victims would they find.

With the magnitude of the disaster apparent, Good Will Fire Company officers immediately summoned additional aid, and the Citizens' Fire Company of nearby Palo Alto responded to the scene with its Mack pumper. Fire Chief George Smith of Pottsville also answered the call for help and dispatched Yorkville Hose Company with its Hahn City Service truck and the West End Fire Company with its Ahrens-Fox Emergency Car from the city. Ambulances from both the Lord and Allen funeral homes in Pottsville were also dispatched to the scene. Firefighters immediately evacuated the passenger cars of the train and commenced a search for any victims. The three trainmen trapped in a baggage car managed a daring escape through a burned-out hole in the vestibule of their car. In an effort to contain the burning gasoline, firefighters applied foam to the blaze. Firefighters also placed several two-and-a-

Firefighting foam covers the ground around the gutted shell of the Mack tractor that pulled the 4,500-gallon gasoline tanker into the railroad crossing that fateful day in Port Carbon in 1949. The driver of the truck was killed. *Schuylkill County Historical Society.*

half-inch hose lines in service to contain the fire in the burning buildings and vehicle.

Firefighters conducting search and rescue operations soon made a gruesome discovery. The truck driver, Clarence Goetz, was killed in the collision. The driver appeared to have died instantly from the explosion; his charred body was burned beyond recognition in the Mack truck cab. Goetz had driven tractor trailer tank trucks for Matlack Inc. for four years and was familiar with this route. Also killed in the accident was Reading Railroad fireman Kenneth Beck of Schuylkill Haven. Beck leaped from the burning locomotive and became engulfed by the fire. Beck succumbed to his injuries twelve hours later in Pottsville Hospital. The engineer,

The local newspaper, the *Pottsville Republican*, announced the accident in Port Carbon in that evening's edition with saturation coverage and dramatic photographs. *Glore collection.*

Charles Moyer, and trainmen William Gift and John Aulenbach were injured and required hospitalization. All injured were transported by Lord and Allen ambulances to nearby Pottsville Hospital. The third and fourth railroad cars of the train, both baggage cars, received the most damage, with the third railcar being virtually destroyed and the fourth railcar badly damaged.

As news of the disaster spread, traffic jams soon developed near the accident scene. State and local police were pressed into service to keep traffic flowing. Also arriving on the scene were inspectors from the United States Postal Service and Reading Railroad officials. Thankfully, all Train No. 91 passengers safely evacuated their passenger railcars. These passengers were soon transferred to a bus from the nearby East Penn Transportation Company and driven to the Tamaqua train station, where another train was assembled to continue the journey. As a wreck train from the Reading Railroad arrived on scene to clear the Reading Railroad mainline and repair the crossing, considerable attention was directed to the second baggage/mail car in the train consist. This car was separated from the others and carefully moved to a siding outside the Pottsville passenger station on East Norwegian Street. Reading Railroad police and Pennsylvania State Police carefully guarded the car while railroad officials searched the contents of the safe in the railcar and postal inspectors attempted to recover any first-class mail not destroyed by the fire.

Unknown to most train crew members, over $300,000, a princely sum in 1949, had been placed in the train safe, destined for banks in Girardville and Trevorton. Railroad officials carefully opened the safe, and all funds, although scorched from the searing heat, were recovered. Unfortunately, most first-class mail was destroyed by the fire. Investigators from the Interstate Commerce Commission in Washington, D.C., conducted an investigation into this accident and delivered its findings in a report dated November 28, 1949. Investigators determined that the accident was caused by the truck driver occupying a rail-highway grade crossing immediately in front of an approaching train. Under the laws of the state of Pennsylvania governing the operation of motor vehicles, the driver of the truck was required to stop the vehicle immediately before it entered the rail-highway grade crossing to determine if he could safety enter the crossing. The hospitalized engineer and trainmen soon recovered from their injuries, never to forget, however, their harrowing experience.

5

NO REST FOR THE WEARY

MAY 31, 1945

The World War II years were challenging for most fire departments in cities and towns throughout the United States. With an all-out government priority afforded to the war effort, new fire apparatus and new firefighting equipment purchases were difficult if not impossible in most locations. Compounding that problem for many communities was a lack of young firefighting manpower, as most of the "brawn" of the fire service enlisted or was drafted into the armed forces. Fire stations were often simply manned by those too old for military service.

In 1945, the fire department of Mahanoy City, Pennsylvania, a thriving Schuylkill County coal town of about thirteen thousand residents, simply had to follow the standard policy for fire departments in most cities and towns during the war: "make do with what you have." Mahanoy City did, however, receive two Civil Defense trailer-drawn five-hundred-gallons-per-minute (GPM) auxiliary fire pumps to supplement the department. In 1945, Mahanoy City boasted five volunteer fire stations: Humane No. 1, Citizens No. 2, Good-American No. 3, West End No. 5 and the Washington Hook & Ladder Company No. 1. While this five-company department served the community diligently during World War II, its mettle was soon to be put to the test. A new, dangerous menace was threatening the peace and safety of Mahanoy City—a "firebug" was on the loose!

THE FIRES BEGIN

In April and May 1945, a rash of fires struck the borough. The sounding of the municipal fire alarm, the local colliery whistle, often during the early morning hours, soon became a regular and dreaded occurrence. Mahanoy City's volunteer firefighters rushed from fire to fire as the arsonist struck mostly an easy target at will—garages. Emboldened by his success, on April 23 and again on May 19, the arsonist moved to a larger target. On both dates, he attempted to burn Saint Casimir's Polish Church Hall on West Maple Street. Only the quick response of the fire department twice saved the structure. Every fire revealed the same source of origin—an oily cotton rag stuffed into a crevice of the building's outer structure and ignited.

When it became apparent that a firebug was waging war on the community, Fire Chief Wassel Govera, a member from the Humane Fire Company, and Police Chief A.P. McLaughlin set up fire watches and asked that the fire stations to be manned. Volunteers staffed the fire stations during the night, and fire watches were established by concerned citizens and police officers during late nights and early mornings, times the arsonist most often commenced his crime. Additionally, the Reading Railroad, which ran virtually through the center of town, furnished railroad police to patrol the tracks and sidings. Still the arsonist struck again with impudence. Who was this incendiarist? Would this criminal graduate to even larger occupied buildings and properties? What was this person's motive? After a half-dozen arson fires during this time frame, Chief Govera telegraphed Captain W.F. Traeger of the Pennsylvania State Police Fire Marshal's Office in Harrisburg seeking assistance. Captain Traeger dispatched several detectives trained in arson fire investigations to Mahanoy City to assist the local police efforts.

May 1945 was recorded as one of the driest months on weather records. Weeks rolled by without a single raindrop recorded in the community. A brief respite in the arsonist's spree occurred from May 20 to May 30, as no fires were reported during this time. However, in the early morning hours of May 31, on a dry and windy Memorial Day, the arsonist struck. This occasion was deemed the "Big One." Snatching some oil-soaked cotton waste from the journal box of a nearby railroad car, the arsonist shoved the cotton into a crevice in a Railroad Street garage behind the Alshultz Wallpaper Store at 125 West Center Street and ignited it. He then returned to his apartment about 2:30 a.m. to await the ensuing excitement.

DISCOVERY

John Coyle, night watchman for the Reading Railroad, was on duty at the Reading Passenger Station at Main and Vine Streets when, looking to the west, discovered an orange glow from a garage building on West Railroad Street. Coyle immediately telephoned the Mahanoy City Police Department. The sergeant on duty dispatched Patrolman Charles Stern in a police car to the area to check on the report of fire. Upon arriving on the scene and witnessing a major fire developing, Patrolman Stern immediately went to Box 21 at West Centre and Catawissa Streets and transmitted the fire alarm at 2:40 a.m. With the sounding of four rounds of Box 21 on the colliery whistle, summoning the fire department once again, the battle commenced.

Fanned by a brisk and steady winds of up to forty miles per hour during the prevailing dry conditions, the fire raged out of control almost immediately. The tall, heavy-timbered buildings of the downtown business district provided an ample source of fuel for the blaze. Fire

Flames march through the frame buildings along the 100 block of West Centre Street as a lone hose stream is directed at the inferno. *Francis Senglar Collection.*

Chief Govera arrived minutes after the alarm sounded, and on seeing the severity and intensity of the fire, he immediately ran to the fire alarm box at Main and Centre Streets and struck four taps on the alarm system, an All-Call signal summoning a response of the entire fire department. Responding firefighters were met with a developing conflagration in their downtown as the wind-driven flames were consuming several buildings in the business district.

Arriving from a few short blocks away, the Humane Fire Company, responding in their 1938 Mack, connected their pumper to the hydrant at Center and Linden Streets. The advancing fiery foe soon threatened their apparatus, forcing the driver to relocate to a hydrant at Centre and Locust Streets. The Citizens Fire Company placed their 1927 American La France pumper in service at the hydrant at Locust and Pine Streets. The Good-American Hose Company immediately took the plug at Main and Centre Streets with their 1939 Hahn pumper. The West End Fire Company, responding from West Centre Street, placed their 1929 Buffalo pumper in service at Pine and Linden Streets. The Washington Hook &

Tremendous radiant heat was generated by the blazing frame buildings. Firemen were forced to retreat ahead of the advancing flames, moving hose lines and fire apparatus to safer and more advantageous positions. *Francis Senglar Collection.*

Hundreds of onlooks gather to view the destruction caused by the fire in Mahanoy City on Memorial Day 1945. A utility company truck operates to the right. Note that fire extended beyond the block of origin during the conflagration. *Francis Senglar Collection.*

Ladder Company raised the aerial ladder of their 1936 Pirsch ladder truck and positioned the truck on West Centre Street for an elevated master stream operation.

FOUR TAPS!

Responding to the All-Call for a full department, the Humane also responded with its reserve pumper, a 1928 American La France, and placed this unit in service at Main and Vine Streets, near the train station. The Washington Hook & Ladder Company sent their 1926 Buffalo/Larrabee pumper to the hydrant at East Centre and Second Streets. Civil Defense five hundred GPM auxiliary pumps, provided by the federal government for such fire emergencies, were trailered from the West

Hose lines continue to operate as spectators gather and utility contractors attempt to restore service to the devastated fire area. *Francis Senglar Collection.*

End and Good-American stations and pressed into service. The West End unit worked from a hydrant at Catawissa and Market Streets and the Good-American unit from a hydrant at Main and Market Streets. With numerous two-and-a-half-inch hose lines in operation, the fire still spread unabated.

A CRY FOR MORE HELP

A mere twenty minutes into the fire, the inferno had virtually consumed the entire 100 block of West Centre Street in the heart of Mahanoy City's business district. Businesses in the path of destruction included Fried's Furniture Store, Kreb's Drug Store, Lutz Lumber Company, Triangle Shoe Store, Friedberg's Department Store and the Alshulz Wallpaper Store. Threatened by the flames were numerous other businesses and residences, including the massive Guinan's Department Store. Fire Chief Govera frantically summoned help from the local Bell Telephone operators to procure assistance from virtually every nearby community, including Tamaqua, Ryan Township, Shenandoah, Gilberton, Frackville, Ashland, Gordon and Centralia. Additionally, local operators telephoned residents threatened by the blaze to notify them to prepare for evacuation. The Citizens Fire Company of Tamaqua dispatched its 1937 Seagrave City Service truck to the fire and "took" the hydrant at Main and Birch Streets. One can only imagine the horrific sight afforded to Tamaqua and Ryan Township firefighters as they crested the Vulcan Hill and looked awestruck at the terrifying inferno awaiting them. ON learning of the severity of the fire, Shenandoah Fire Chief Adam Balkiewicz arrived with two Shenandoah units to fight the blaze: the Columbia and his own company, the Polish American. The Columbia, responding in their 1921 American La France, was ordered by Chief Govera to provide manpower where needed and to patrol the fire area. The Polish American with their 1941 Mack pumper drafted water from the Mahanoy Creek at Market Street between Linden and Catawissa Streets.

MORE ASSISTANCE ARRIVES

The Gilberton Ducktowners, responding to the call for help, connected their 1942 Diamond T fire truck to the hydrant at Catawissa and Pine Streets and put several hose lines into operation. The Washington Fire Company responded with Chief John Snyder in their 1933 Seagraves. This pumper was put into service at Main and Mahanoy Streets. The Citizens Fire Company of Gordon, arriving in their 1937 Chevrolet/ Darley pumper, was directed to Market Street between Linden and Locust to draft from the Mahanoy Creek. The Altamont Fire Company of Frackville took the hydrant at Pine and A Streets with their 1939 Hahn. The newly organized Ryan Township Fire Company with their 1927 Stutz Chemical truck were utilized for manpower and fire patrol. The Centralia Fire Company with its 1939 Hahn came all the way from Columbia County. This pumper pumped from a plug at Linden and Mahanoy Streets until a bearing failure occurred. During the height of the fire, Chief Govera reported twenty-six two-and-a-half-hose lines were in operation. Embers from the fire appeared in Locust Valley, over five miles from the fire.

Top: A great view looking generally to the northeast over the ruins of the Memorial Day Fire in 1945. The Washington Hook & Ladder truck is operating on the remains of the buildings where the fire jumped Linden Street. *Bill Kates photo, Mahanoy Area Historical Society.*

Bottom: Citizens view the ruins of the Memorial Day fire looking north toward Railroad Street. *Mary Ambrose photo, Mahanoy Area Historical Society.*

Opposite: Perhaps the most familiar photos from the Memorial Day fire, this view looks northwest and captures the devastation across several blocks. Humane's Mack pumpers operates in the lower portion of the photo. *Joe Conrad photo, Francis Senglar Collection.*

AFTERMATH

By daybreak, the wind had died down and firefighters finally gained control of the blaze; however, local firefighters continued to wet down hotspots for many additional hours. The destruction was incredible: two and a half blocks of the business district of Mahanoy City were virtually leveled by the firestorm. Thirty-eight businesses were destroyed, including the large Guinan's Department Store and Snyder Apartment building. Thirty-eight families lost not only their homes but also all of their possessions. Over two hundred people were now homeless. The fire made headlines in newspapers across the country and even appeared in the military's *Stars and Stripes* publication, where many servicemen from throughout the area learned about the fire. Miraculously, no deaths were directly attributed to the fire itself. Many firefighters were treated for injuries incurred during their firefighting efforts.

A SUSPECT EMERGES

In comparing notes, police investigators and fire officials began to focus on a prime arson candidate: Joseph Giblin, a.k.a. Joseph Mullahey. Giblin, who originally hailed from nearby Shenandoah, was spotted in the crowd of bystanders at multiple arson fires. Moreover, Giblin, a local handyman and dishwasher, lived in a basement apartment below Chef's Restaurant on East Centre Street, where he was employed. Giblin had previously worked for the Reading Railroad, thus having the knowledge of extracting the oily cotton rags from the journal boxes of railroad cars, the source of origin at every recent fire. On the morning of the Memorial Day Fire, Giblin was spotted near Centre Street. Police Chief McLaughlin called out to him, but Giblin turned the corner onto Market Street and kept walking. McLaughlin and another officer caught up to Giblin and called out to him again. This time Giblin turned back to the chief and asked if he wanted him. McLaughlin and Officer Stern asked Giblin to return to police headquarters for questioning.

CONFESSION

Soon after arriving at the Mahanoy City Police Department on East Pine Street and after initial questioning by Police Chief McLaughlin, Joseph Giblin broke down into tears and confessed to setting this fire. Additionally, Giblin confessed to setting seven earlier fires in the borough, showing police officials how he set the fires, using oily cotton rags from the journal boxes of nearby railroad cars. Giblin described how he turned in the fire alarm after the first three fires that he set but then allowed residents to transmit the alarm. Giblin stated that he did not know why he set the fires but planned on turning himself in. Fire Chief Wassel Govera wrote down Giblin's confession and had Giblin sign the confession, which was turned over to the Pennsylvania State Police. Giblin was arraigned before a local justice of the peace and was held without bail in the Schuylkill County Prison. On June 1, Giblin was arraigned by Schuylkill County Judge Vincent Dalton and given ten to twenty years for each count of arson. Giblin served his term in the Eastern State Penitentiary in Philadelphia and died in prison in 1973.

6

FLIGHT TO OBLIVION

JUNE 17, 1948

United Airlines Flight 624 was a regularly scheduled flight originating from Lindberg Field, San Diego, California, with stops in Los Angeles and Chicago en route to La Guardia Airport in New York City. The airplane for Thursday, June 17, 1948, was a Douglas DC-6, a four-engine, propeller-driven plane and part of a fleet of Douglas DC-6 aircraft used by United Airlines. Captain for the flight was George Warner, a veteran pilot for United Airlines. The flight departed from San Diego on time.

The airplane, named Mainliner Utah, arrived in Chicago from Los Angeles at 9:52 a.m. The aircraft departed Chicago fifty-two minutes later, destined for New York City, with thirty-nine passengers and four crew members aboard. After departing Chicago, the plane climbed to its planned altitude of seventeen thousand feet. As the aircraft crossed central Pennsylvania at an estimated speed of three hundred miles per hour, Captain Warner began the plane's initial routine descent to eleven thousand feet as part of its approach to the La Guardia Airport in New York City.

Soon afterward, trouble erupted. The forward cargo hold fire alarm illuminated, leading the flight crew to believe that a fire had developed in that cargo area. Although a later investigation showed that the alarm was a false activation, the crew decided to discharge the carbon dioxide (CO_2) fire suppression system into that hold to try to extinguish the possible fire. While proper airline operating procedures called for opening the cabin pressure relief valves prior to discharging the CO_2 cylinders, to allow for venting of the CO_2 gas buildup in the cabin and cockpit, there was no evidence that the crew ever opened the relief valves.

Individuals survey some of the wreckage of Flight 624 as the electrical transformer, which was struck by the right wing of the plane, is clearly visible. *Tom Dempsey Sr. Collection*

Consequently, investigators from the Civil Aeronautics Board believed that the CO_2 gas released from the fire extinguishers seeped back into the cockpit from the front cargo hold and apparently incapacitated the flight crew. The hazardous concentrations of CO_2 gas would gradually reduce the flight crew's consciousness into a state of unconsciousness. An emergency descent was initiated, and the plane continued to lose altitude. Descending into the Appalachian Mountains of central Pennsylvania, the plane reportedly flew over the city of Shamokin at an altitude of only two hundred feet above the ground.

The troubled aircraft continued several miles eastward, passing over the Northumberland County coal region communities of Kulpmont and Mount Carmel. Residents and motorists throughout this area reported hearing and seeing the airplane in its downward descent. Near the small mining village of Wilburton, close to the Schuylkill/Columbia County line, the starboard wing of the DC-6 dipped toward the ground and struck a sixty-six-thousand-volt electrical transformer, feeding power to the nearby Midvalley Colliery of the Hazle Brook Coal Company. A tremendous explosion rocked the area, and the DC-6 burst into a skyward ball of fire as it crashed to the ground. Stunned employees of the coal company literally ran for their lives. The time was 1:40 p.m.

On realizing the disaster that just unfolded before them, coal company officials immediately began telephoning police, fire and ambulance responders to the stricken area. The scene was one of utter destruction and unspeakable horror. Across several hundred square yards adjoining the Midvalley Colliery lay fragments of the DC-6 aircraft and dozens of bodies and body parts and personal belongings. Fires continued to rage in the blown-out engines of the aircraft and in the trees and brush in the affected area. News of the disaster spread quickly. First of the responders to arrive on the scene was the Wilburton Fire Company No. 1 in their 1946 Chevrolet fire truck. They were soon joined by fire companies from Mount Carmel, Centralia and Ashland. Fire Chief John Snyder of Ashland assumed command and directed firefighting operations over the vast burning area.

Ambulances from Mount Carmel, Ashland and the Hazle Brook Coal Company arrived on the scene shortly afterward. State police from the Shamokin and Bloomsburg barracks soon converged on the area as well. Catholic priests from Saint Ignatius Parish in nearby Centralia traversed the grounds, administering last rites to the victims. There were no survivors. A morgue was set up in the Stutz Funeral Home of Centralia, and ambulances transported bodies and body parts to that location.

The ground surrounding the Midvalley Colliery shows the devastation from the crash of the Douglas DC-6 airliner as the wreckage continues to smolder. *Tom Dempsey Sr. Collection.*

Radio announcer Ed Darlington of Station WCNR of Bloomsburg arrived and began live radio broadcasts from the crash scene. Salvation Army members from Mount Carmel and Shamokin prepared meals and refreshments for the numerous first responders who continued to arrive. As news of the disaster was announced on national news venues, families and friends of the airplane's passengers rushed to the area in search of any survivors. Over twenty-five state police were needed to control traffic and prevent looting at the disaster area. State police closed the main highway through Wilburton for many hours during recovery operations. During the time of the crash, the National Republican Convention was commencing in Philadelphia. Many convention delegates were fearful that Republican attendees were among the victims.

With a death toll of forty-three, the crash of United Airlines Flight 624 on Thursday, June 17, 1948, ranked as the fourth-worst commercial airline disaster in United States' history at that time. Notable victims of the catastrophe included Broadway theater impresario Earl Carroll; actress Beryl Wallace; Henry L. Jackson, fashion editor of *Collier's Weekly* magazine and co-founder of *Esquire* magazine; and Venita Vardon Oakley, the former wife of actor Jack Oakley. The Civil Aeronautics Board concluded that the probable cause of this accident was the incapacitation of the crew by a concentration of CO_2 gas in the cockpit. A 1946 Chevrolet pumper, the first emergency apparatus to arrive at the disaster scene, is now part of the Schuylkill Historical Fire Society Museum collection in Shenandoah, Pennsylvania.

7

NO WORK TOMORROW!

MAY 19, 1956

The repeated staccato blasts of the Reading Railroad steam locomotive pierced the early Saturday morning air of Pine Grove. The railroad engineer, hauling a load of empty coal hoppers to nearby Lorberry Junction, surely wanted to wake the dead. Something had to be wrong. Soloman Barr, plant foreman of the Garden State Tannery Company, working third shift that morning, heard the blasts and decided to investigate. Barr quickly discovered what the Reading engineer had already found—a fire was burning out of control between the buffing and pasting rooms near the northern end of the tannery. Barr quickly telephoned Buell Lengle, on-duty taxi driver in downtown Pine Grove, who drove to the nearby Hose, Hook and Ladder Fire Company No. 1 (HH&L) and sounded the town fire alarm. The time was 3:15 a.m.

The Garden State Tannery was an immense complex of several large adjoining buildings of heavy timber and brick masonry construction, two and a half stories tall, along North Tulpehocken Street in Pine Grove. The main building was over one thousand feet in length. The tannery, originally called the Pine Grove Tanning Company, first began operation in 1906 and employed 340 workers from throughout the Pine Grove area at the time of the fire. With a weekly payroll of over $30,000, the business was a major contributor to the economy of western Schuylkill County. The tannery supplied leather for numerous enterprises, including the automotive and shoe industries. At the time of the fire, Garden State Tannery reportedly had orders for 775,000 feet of leather; another company expansion was being planned, and over $100,000 was budgeted for that project.

Responding from its headquarters on Mifflin Street in Pine Grove Borough was the HH&L Fire Company in its Mack pumper. Also in response were members of the North End Fire Company, just north of the borough line in Pine Grove Township, in their Ford pumper. Both fire companies were confronted with a daunting task on arrival at the scene: fed by vast amounts of paints, thinners, lacquers and chemicals stored in the buffing and pasting rooms, the fire was now raging out of control and consuming an entire section of the main building of the tannery. Also threatened was the nearby Fox-Knapp Factory. Shocked by the sheer size of the fire already, Pine Grove businessman Ernest Gottschall requested the local Bell Telephone operator to summon help from all neighboring communities.

Pine Grove firefighters, using nearby fire hydrants, attempted to stop the fire in the main tannery building with several two-and-a-half-inch hose lines. Those efforts became futile as the fire continued to gain intensity and spread rapidly. Flames were reportedly already shooting over two hundred feet

A portion of the massive Garden State Tanning complex is virtually consumed as flames light the night sky. *Pine Grove Hose, Hook, & Ladder Fire Company Collection.*

Nighttime flames illustrate the varying heights and building construction features of the sprawling Garden State Tanning facility. *Pine Grove Hose, Hook, & Ladder Fire Company Collection.*

into the sky, and firefighters were forced to make a hasty retreat due to the intense heat. The extreme radiant heat and burning embers now threatened residential homes along North Tulpehocken Street, and several homes were scorched. Many homeowners removed furnishings to a safer location; others manned garden hoses to cool down the backs of their homes. The first arriving mutual aid fire companies from Ravine, Tremont and Suedburg began drafting water from the nearby Swatara Creek and pumping it to the scene of the conflagration.

Within two hours after the fire alarm sounded, the fire had consumed the entire main building of the tannery and continued to spread quickly. That building housed the main offices, tanning department, beam house, drum room and the buffing and pasting rooms. The blaze now moved unabated to adjoining buildings in the massive tannery complex. Periodic explosions enhanced the unfolding drama as containers of paints and chemicals ignited. Additional out-of-town fire companies continued to arrive at the scene and soon set up drafting sites along two small tributaries feeding into the Swatara Creek. These companies included Schuylkill Haven, Minersville, Cressona, Auburn, Orwin and Reinerton. The Liberty Hose Company of Williamstown arrived from

An individual peers over the devastation the flames left behind at the tannery. He appears to be looking over a gondola along the railroad siding at the facility. *Pine Grove Hose, Hook, & Ladder Fire Company Collection.*

Dauphin County. Fire Chief George Smith of Pottsville, answering the call for help, sent the American Hose Company and the Humane Fire Company, the city's biggest pumpers, to the fire scene. A total of eleven communities answered the call for help and sent manpower and equipment to fight the blaze.

Pennsylvania Power & Light lineman Franklin Bendt of Tremont was a hero of this disaster. Working with a four-man crew, Bendt climbed a burning utility pole and, using a hand fire extinguisher, put out a fire near a burning transformer, thus keeping the transformer and power lines in service. Although the community was without power for about two hours, a much longer power outage would have occurred without Bendt's heroic actions. State and local police stopped traffic at Pottsville and Tulpehocken Streets; smoke described as thick as fog limited visibility along Route 443 in the borough. At the height of the fire, flames reportedly were visible in Friedensburg, eleven miles east of Pine Grove.

By 7:15 a.m. four hours after the fire alarm sounded, the tannery complex had virtually been leveled. Firefighters continued to pour large quantities of water onto the burning debris, but despite their valiant efforts, the tannery was no more. The few small buildings to survive the holocaust were a maintenance shop and a small warehouse. Tannery officials, led

What appears to be a Ford dump truck stands parked next to the still-standing masonry walls of the tannery complex, which serve as a shell to the gutted plant. *Pine Grove Hose, Hook, & Ladder Fire Company Collection.*

With a loss of over $1 million, company officials made the decision to not rebuild the plant. Firemen from eleven communities assisted Pine Grove fire companies in battling what was one of the largest fires in Schuylkill County history. *Pine Grove Hose, Hook, & Ladder Fire Company Collection.*

by Superintendent A. Klastow and the Executive Board, gathered near the site of the factory that morning to view firsthand the destruction and to contemplate future plans. With losses over $1 million, a final decision was made not to rebuild. May 19, 1956, marked one of the largest fires in Schuylkill County history.

8

DAY OF INFAMY

JUNE 2, 1959

Roger Schrope was one happy schoolboy—and rightfully so. The end of the school year was just around the corner, and another long summer vacation full of fun and adventure would soon commence. Despite the rainy weather, Tuesday, June 2, started off as any typical day with a long school bus ride from his home in Molino to his Blue Mountain School District building in Cressona. A stop was made along Route 122 near the Red Church about 8 a.m. at the Herb house to pick up a pupil, one of Roger's classmates. And then tragedy struck.

Joseph Wharton of Peckville, a truck driver for Sun Gas Marketers of Scranton, began his workday at 4:30 a.m. at truck loading facility in Marcus Hook, Pennsylvania. After checking out his Mack tractor and tank trailer, he was ready to haul a load of seven thousand gallons of liquid propane to the Correal Mining Company at St. Clair. Joe calculated that the long ride north on Route 122 should get him to the worksite in the mine fields about 9:00 a.m. Joe would never make his delivery that day.

Walter Williams of Reading, a driver for Branch Motor Express, was also heading north on Route 122 with cartons of textiles for the Phillips Jones Corporation, a local shirt factory. Driving in a rainstorm, Williams soon confronted stopped traffic directly in front of him. Williams, unable to stop his tractor trailer, skidded on the rain-slick highway and struck the trailer of the Wharton truck, loaded with liquid propane. The Wharton truck had stopped on Route 122 for a school bus picking up a passenger. An engine fire ensued from Williams's damaged tractor and soon began to engulf the propane trailer.

Steam continues to rise from both the roadway and the Branch tractor-trailer following the explosion. *Schuylkill County Historical Society.*

Roger, on hearing the collision, stuck his head out the window of the school bus and immediately pulled it back as a thermal wave from the truck fire enveloped the bus. School bus driver Russell Klahr of Schuylkill Haven, hearing the truck accident directly behind his bus and seeing the tractor burst into flames, immediately drove his busload of children out of harm's way. A second Blue Mountain school bus, driven by Ronald Kramer of Auburn, was following the Williams tractor trailer. Upon seeing the fire and fearing an explosion, Kramer made a U-turn with his bus and drove through a farmer's field onto a dirt road and into Orwigsburg, thus averting a potential disaster.

At 8:05 a.m., the house sirens began to wail in Orwigsburg and Deer Lake, summoning volunteer firefighters from both communities as reports began arriving announcing a truck fire on State Highway 122 near Zion's Red Church, about one mile south of Orwigsburg. Friendship Hose Company No. 1 of Orwigsburg responded from its Mifflin Street station with its 1957 Ford pumper and Fire Chief James Marotte. As additional help arrived at the station, the company's second engine, a 1949 Chevrolet/Oren pumper,

The shattered chassis is all that remains of the Sun Company propane tanker following the devastation explosion. *Schuylkill County Historical Society.*

was dispatched to the scene. The Deer Lake Fire Company sent its 1948 Diamond T pumper to the fire.

After arriving at the scene and assessing the situation, Pennsylvania State Policeman Earl Klinger from the Schuylkill Haven barracks closed Route 122 for safety concerns. Chief Marotte began directing firefighting efforts to the nearby Herb house as severe radiant heat from the trailer fire threatened the home. Firefighters, while concerned with the flames enveloping the propane tank, believed that so long as the tank was venting, no explosion would occur. With additional help needed at the scene, Chief Marotte made a call to Schuylkill Haven, summoning additional firefighting assistance. Schuylkill Haven sent the Rainbow Hose Company No. 1 with its 1949 Seagrave City Service truck and Liberty Fire Company No. 4 with its 1957 Mack pumper to the scene.

Approximately thirty-seven minutes into the incident, the explosion occurred. Known today as a BLEVE, a boiling liquid escaping vapor explosion, the blast tore the tank off its frame and launched it, like a rocket, off the stone wall of the Red Church and into a crowd of bystanders

Above: Bell Telephone Company vehicles are in the foreground as the utility works to restore phone service following the accident. In the background can be seen the shattered stone wall of the "Red Church" as well as the charred remains of the Branch freight truck. *Schuylkill County Historical Society.*

Opposite, top: The Friendship Hose Company of Orwigsburg 1957 Ford-Oren pumper was one of the first to arrive at the tragic 1959 propane tanker explosion. The pumper is shown only three months after the fire participating in a parade in Pottsville in September 1959. *Glore collection.*

Opposite, bottom: Debris and portions of the shattered propane tanker litter then-Route 122 (today's State Route 61) following the devastating explosion that claimed a dozen lives. The rear of the Rainbow Hose Company of Schuylkill Haven's 1951 Seagrave city service truck can be seen and, farther south on the highway, Liberty Fire Company of Schuylkill Haven's 1957 B Model Mack pumper operating closer to the actual crash site. *Schuylkill County Historical Society.*

located several hundred feet away near the road to Orwigsburg. The blast was tremendous, breaking windows in Orwigsburg, over a mile away, and snapping utility poles along the highway. Power and telephone lines were severed, affecting a vast area of southern Schuylkill County and beyond, from Pottsville to the Philadelphia and Harrisburg areas.

The explosion killed and injured dozens of victims, turning the accident area into what was described by Dr. Wagner, an Orwigsburg physician,

Above: A close-up view of the remains of the propane tank that caused the carnage as it rocketed up the highway. *Schuylkill County Historical Society.*

Opposite, top: Time stood still. Wristwatch recovered from one of the victims of the blast. *Schuylkill County Historical Society.*

Opposite, bottom: Local funeral homes go about the grim work of removing the dead. *Schuylkill County Historical Society.*

as a war battlefield scene. Ambulances were summoned from as far away as Pottsville, Schuylkill Haven and Hamburg, and station wagons were commandeered by arriving state police to transport the injured to local hospitals. Additionally, Pottsville sent its 1937 Ahrens-Fox emergency car from the West End Fire Company. All available state police from the Schuylkill Haven barracks were summoned to the disaster scene in addition to fire police from Deer Lake, Orwigsburg and Schuylkill Haven. With telephone lines severed, the additional calls for aid were sent via FM radio, an early use of this means of communication for an emergency. As news of the tragedy spread, traffic on Route 122 became backed up for miles as people came to view the site of the disaster.

The aftermath: twelve people were killed in the explosion, including two firefighters: Earl Hillbish, a member of the Friendship Hose Company of Orwigsburg, and James Leitzel of the Rescue Hook and Ladder Company

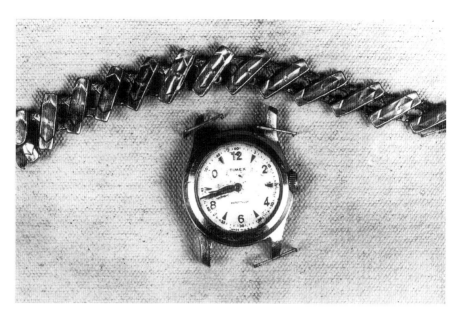

The local *Pottsville Republican* newspaper devoted full front-page coverage to the horrific incident.

of Shenandoah, who stopped to render aid. One of the fatally injured, whose remains were incomplete, was never identified. Additionally, eleven people were injured, several seriously, and transported to hospitals in Pottsville and Reading. Adam Faust, another Friendship Hose Company member, who later served as the fire chief of Orwigsburg, remained unconscious for three days after the blast but fully recovered from his internal injuries. This incident made national and international news and prompted safety training courses and safer technology in the transportation of propane.

9

PENN-VAL DYEING COMPANY FIRE

MARCH 7, 1957

On Thursday, March 7, 1957, sometime after 11:00 a.m., workers at the Penn-Val Dyeing Company on Berne Street in Schuylkill Haven started smelling smoke. An investigation soon determined a fire was burning near the center of the large factory in the drying area of the first floor. Company officials soon placed a hurried call to the borough office on Dock Street, and a general fire alarm was transmitted at 11:15 a.m. Responding were the three companies of the Schuylkill Haven Fire Department: Rainbow No. 1, Schuylkill No. 2 and Liberty No. 4.

Penn-Val Dyeing Company was a subsidiary company of Argo Mills Knitting and Bleachery Inc. and operated out of a massive four-story L-shaped brick structure on the western edge of the borough. At the time of the fire, Penn-Val employed approximately seventy-five workers in this plant. First responding companies connected to hydrants on Berne Street, attempting to prevent the fire from gaining headway. Their efforts were soon thwarted by low water pressure and low water volume from the nearby hydrants.

Arriving in the early stages of the fire, Schuylkill Haven Fire Chief Claude Sausser soon recognized the potential severity of the situation as the fire quickly began to spread. Ironically, company officials had installed new machinery in that section of the factory just four days earlier. As plant foremen were evacuating the factory, Chief Sausser immediately placed a call for assistance to the nearby communities of Cressona, Orwigsburg and the City of Pottsville. As workers were leaving the building, dense smoke soon enveloped the area. Plant foremen began to check if all employees had exited the building. Officials soon determined that two employees were still missing.

Schuylkill Haven firefighters quickly located a missing worker on the second floor of the factory and were able to escort him to safety through a rear stairway. The second missing employee soon appeared at a window on the third floor near the center of the structure. Chief Sausser ordered

With numerous hose lines in the street, firefighters raise a wooden ground ladder at the Penn-Val Dyeing building fire in 1957. *Schuylkill Historical Fire Society Collection.*

Flames engulf the rear of the Penn-Val Dyeing complex, threatening nearby wood frame garages and homes. *Schuylkill Historical Fire Society Collection.*

members of the Rainbow Hose Company to raise their wooden Bangor ladder from their 1951 Seagrave City Service truck to that window and rescue the worker. Rainbow members went to work quickly and successfully rescued the final missing worker with their large extension ladder.

With a poor water supply available from the Berne Street hydrants, Chief Sausser sent pumpers to the nearby Stoyer's Dam to draft water from that location. Soon five pumpers were supplying multiple hose lines across Columbia Avenue (Route 443) to the fire, which continued to gain intensity. Additionally, Chief Sausser requested portable pumps be pressed into service along the Schuylkill River near the Columbia Avenue Bridge. With a large flammable inventory in the building, the fire steadily grew to a conflagration, with embers and firebrands threatening numerous homes adjacent to the factory. Chief Sausser described the fire as the hottest and certainly one of the worst fires in Schuylkill Haven history.

As additional help from surrounding communities began to arrive, these units were immediately placed in service at the fire scene. Chief George Smith of Pottsville sent the American Hose Company and Yorkville Hose Company to assist. These companies set up multiple hose lines to protect the numerous row homes adjacent to the burning factory. The Cressona and Orwigsburg companies helped in the drafting operation from Stoyer's Dam. They were soon joined by the North End Fire Company of Pine Grove, which also responded to the scene. Despite these valiant efforts, the fire soon engulfed the entire four-story factory building.

A second dramatic rescue occurred as a crumbling brick wall from the factory complex collapsed and buried firefighter Therald Bolton, a member of the Schuylkill Hose Company No. 2. Firefighters successfully dug out

Schuylkill Haven firemen, along with the mutual aid companies, direct hose streams into the upper floors of the Penn-Val Dyeing building. *Schuylkill Historical Fire Society Collection.*

The Liberty Fire Company of Schuylkill Haven operates the company's 1927 Hahn pumper at a fire hydrant on Berne Street during the fire. *Schuylkill Historical Fire Society Collection.*

the injured Bolton and removed him to a safe area. Dr. John Schantz of Schuylkill Haven treated Bolton at the scene for head injuries; Bolton was then transported by ambulance to Pottsville Hospital for additional treatment and observation. Firefighter John J. Reilly, a member of the American Hose Company No. 2 of Pottsville, reportedly fractured his hand and was treated at the Good Samaritan Hospital and released. Dr. Schantz also treated several other firefighters on scene for minor injuries.

Despite all the hose lines that were placed into service, firefighting efforts continued all afternoon and into the night. Chief Sausser declared that Stoyer's Dam was "worth a billion dollars" that day, as water from the drafting efforts at the dam helped save many nearby homes and properties. Chief Sausser ordered the Liberty Fire Company No. 4 to stay in service all night long. Several rekindles were quickly contained by the Liberty members.

After over twenty-four hours of battling the blaze, local firefighters were finally released from the scene. While no final dollar loss amount was ever provided, company officials estimated their loss at over $1 million. Additionally, approximately seventy-five employees lost their jobs that day, a major economic blow to the community.

10

FIRE AND ICE

JANUARY 19, 1971

Ernest Eichenbaum operated the Pottsville Showcase and Equipment Company near the lower part of Minersville and Laurel Streets. The building in which he operated became a victim of progress and was razed as part of the Minersville Street Redevelopment Project. In 1964, he moved his business to the large, imposing three-story building of ordinary construction that was located at 300 North Third Street—on the northeast corner of the intersection at Third and West Race Streets.

This building was originally built as a soap factory following a massive fire in the block in 1873. It had also housed the Hoffman Furniture Store. It later served as an automobile dealership, first as Reber Chevrolet and later as Troutman Pontiac. The Showcase building stood less than a block from the new Humane Fire Company firehouse at Third Street and Laurel Boulevard. Humane's original firehouse at the foot of Laurel Street at Third also became a victim of the Minersville Street Redevelopment project. A parking lot and Humane Alley separated the firehouse and the Showcase building. The Pottsville Showcase and Equipment Company supplied furnishings and other necessary equipment for restaurants, bars and so on.

Francis Cremia worked at the relatively new Pottsville Post Office complex in the 400 block of North Centre Street. Early on Tuesday morning, January 19, 1971, he and several other Postal employees decided to head to a local diner for their night shift meal. As they exited the post office shortly after 2:30 a.m., they were met by the biting cold. Temperatures at that early morning

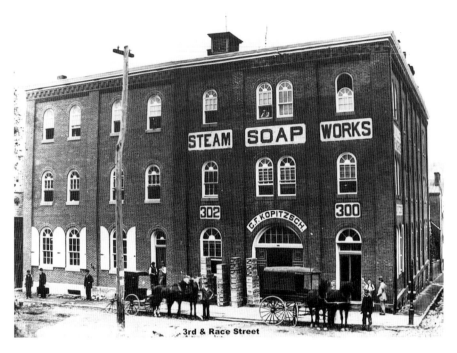

The Kopitzsch Soap Works building as it looked in the late nineteenth Century. This building would come to house the Pottsville Showcase & Equipment Company restaurant supply store later in the twentieth century. *Schuylkill County Historical Society Collection.*

hour hovered near 0 degrees. Pulling collars to cheeks, they rounded the corner at Third and Laurel Boulevard—directly in front of the Humane Fire Company—and were stopped dead in their tracks. With eyes widening, they discovered smoke pouring from the nearly half-block-long Pottsville Showcase building just ahead. Cremia quickly raced to turn in the alarm. At 02:47 a.m., Box 43 began to bang-in on the Gamewell house gongs in the eight Pottsville firehouses as well as at city hall. In short order, the cold, silent night air was pierced by the wailing house sirens.

Driving Good Intent's 1958 Oren 750-GPM pumper, Foreman Dennis McCabe wheeled the engine onto to North Third Street from West Market. Smoke was hanging heavy in the area from the fire two blocks away. As he crossed West Arch Street, a wind shift dropped the smoke level down to the street. McCabe slowed the handsome pumper to a crawl and inched the rig forward until he approached the intersection with West Race. He left room for Phoenix's 1959 American LaFrance one-hundred-foot tractor-drawn aerial ladder truck to position in front of the building.

Thankfully, it was a relatively short ride in the open cab and open tiller seat of the Phoenix's ladder truck that bitterly cold morning.

Fire Chief Andy Hoke arrived on scene and realized quickly that he was going to be facing the largest fire to that point in his thirteen-year career. His assistant chiefs at the time of the fire were Bill Stephenson (Good Will Fire Company), Donald "Doc" Bound (West End Hose Company) and Jake Gerace (Yorkville Hose & Fire Company). Wearing self-contained breathing apparatus (SCBA) and some filter-type masks, firefighters tried repeatedly to press an interior attack with both booster lines and one-and-a-half-inch hand lines. As firefighters forced entry and vented, conditions rapidly deteriorated, and it became apparent to Hoke that the building would be doomed. Firefighters were withdrawn from the building and exterior operations begun. At 03:10 a.m., Hoke transmitted a second alarm. This brought the remaining apparatus still in city fire stations to the scene. Two-and-a-half-inch supply lines were laid from virtually every hydrant in the vicinity.

Smoke pours from the building as the Phoenix Fire Company prepares the ladder pipe on their 1959 American LaFrance one-hundred-foot tractor-drawn aerial ladder truck on North Third Street. The Good Will Fire Company operates with their 1963 GMC/American high-pressure pumper. *Phoenix Fire Engine Company No. 2 Collection.*

West End positioned their 1960 Seagrave sixty-five-foot 750-GPM quint on the north (B Side) of the fire building in the parking lot. West End's 1963 Seagrave 750-GPM pumper obtained a water supply and pumped to the quint.

Firefighter Timmy Ellison climbed the extended aerial to operate the ladder pipe. He hydraulically vented the small window just below the roof peak leading to the attic area. Firefighter George Glore, coauthor Michael Glore's father, positioned himself on the aerial ladder below Ellison to facilitate communication between the tip and the turntable. After Ellison operated the pipe along the roofline, the biting cold and smoke condition took their toll on him. He yelled to Glore that he was going to come down to take a break. When they arrived on the turntable, Glore proceed to the tip. Arriving at the tip and squinting through tearing eyes, Glore lowered the pipe from the roofline. Reaching out, he tightened the pattern on the Akron Black Widow fog tip to a straight stream and drove the stream into the inky smoke that was now churning from the attic window. Firefighters rotated at the tip throughout the night—most were eventually equipped with self-contained breathing apparatus. As each climbed down the ladder, they were largely coated in ice. By 3:40 a.m., fire was showing from numerous windows in the building, and by 3:50 a.m., fire had broken through the roof.

Firefighters poured water into the building from various access points. The water quickly froze everywhere. Chief Hoke knew that his men were taking a beating. He also knew that all of his firefighting resources were at the scene. He requested mutual aid from the Schuylkill Haven Fire Department. Schuylkill Haven Liberty and Schuylkill Hose each sent a pumper and were stationed at the Good Intent Fire Company and the nearby Humane Fire Company. The Rainbow Fire Company initially started out with a piece of apparatus (one of the company's 1951 Seagrave rigs), but it was found that the brakes were faulty. Rainbow firemen accompanied the other two companies to Pottsville. The firefighters from the Rainbow Hose Company of Schuylkill Haven made their way from the Humane firehouse to assist and relieve Pottsville firefighters. In one instance, Haven firefighters assumed the operation of a two-and-a-half-inch handline by simply placing their hands into the gloves worn by Pottsville firefighters that were frozen to the nozzle.

The Humane Fire Company was used to rehabilitate firefighters who were literally frozen in their turnout gear. Humane Fire Company Ladies Auxiliary members used electric hair dryers to thaw the turnout coat closures of the firefighters. Having the new Humane building so close allowed freezing and weary firefighters to thaw out and get a cup of coffee—or perhaps something a little stronger—and a donut prior to returning to the fireground.

Perched atop the sixty-five-foot aerial ladder on the West End Hose Company's 1960 Seagrave quint, coauthor Michael Glore's father, George Glore, directs a stream from the ladder pipe into the Pottsville Showcase building. *Glore collection.*

Taken from in front of the Humane Fire Company's quarters, fire apparatus from (*left to right*) Humane, West End, and Greenwood Hill operate in the bitterly cold early morning hours at the Pottsville Showcase fire in 1971. *Glore collection.*

Throughout the night, firefighters continued to pour water on the blazing Showcase building. Phoenix operated their ladder pipe on the Third Street side of the fire building. Yorkville firefighters raised their Bangor ladder to the exposed three-story occupied multiple dwelling of ordinary construction on the southeast corner of Third and West Race Streets. A handline was advanced to the roof of that building to direct into the Showcase. This apartment building was undamaged and still stands today. Also exposed in the rear was a large two-and-a-half-story private dwelling and garage on the northwest corner of Second and West Race Streets. This home was not damaged by the fire, as firefighters had hose lines in position to protect it from the flying embers. Several garages in the rear alley also escaped fire damage. The American Hose Company operated in the rear off West Race Street with the company's venerable American LaFrance 700 series pumpers, including "Bertha"—the company's 1948 1500-GPM pumper that supplied water from Centre Street.

The lower level of the Showcase building was used as garage space and was rented by residents of the neighborhood. Of the nine vehicles in the garage at the time of the fire, seven were destroyed. The Showcase truck and one automobile were saved. At one point, when the interior of the building began to collapse, car horns began sounding from the garage area, creating a prolonged annoyance.

City Street Department crews were also on scene to spread anti-skid material, as there was a very large ice accumulation. Pennsylvania Power & Light crews secured power to the Showcase building. Salvation Army personnel were also on hand and provided hot coffee to the weary firemen.

Ice remains coated on the Phoenix Fire Company's American LaFrance aerial ladder truck after the company had returned to quarters that morning. Note the hose that supplied the ladder pipe still frozen to the aerial ladder. *Phoenix Fire Engine Company No. 2 Collection.*

The fire was placed under control at seven o'clock that morning. However, it continued to flare up for some time. For the next day and a half, fire companies rotated being on scene and pouring water into the smoldering ruins. The last water was applied on Thursday morning, January 21.

Wrapping up from the scene provided an additional challenge for firefighters, as all apparatus and equipment were ice-encrusted. The Good Intent kept a bottle of whiskey on their 1958 Oren pumper to provide instant warmth at bitterly cold fire scenes. That morning, however, Engineer Dale Ward used the whiskey on the windshield of the pumper to thaw the ice in order to return to quarters. Phoenix did not return to quarters until noon that day. The stories of the firefighting efforts and the battle against the elements that night have become legendary in the Pottsville Fire Department. The Showcase fire was for that generation of firefighters what the Chip Factory fire (Reiland's—Ninth and Laurel) was for the next generation or what Pierce Street is for our generation. Andy Hoke cited the Pottsville Showcase fire and the Pottsville Club fire (300 Block Mahantongo) in 1974 as the two most challenging fires of his seventeen-year career. The Schuylkill County Adult Probation offices currently occupy the site where the Pottsville Showcase building once stood.

The cause of the fire is officially listed as "undetermined."

11

NO MATINEE TOMORROW

DECEMBER 27, 1965

Attending the afternoon matinees at the Strand Theater was a weekly ritual for hundreds of children in the Shenandoah area in the 1960s. With the Christmas season of 1965 still in full swing, an even larger crowd of youngsters was on hand for the premiere showing of *Pinocchio in Outer Space* for Monday, December 27. The matinee commenced at 1:00 p.m. with several Tom and Jerry cartoons before Pinocchio appeared on the silver screen. About thirty minutes into the program, ominous signs of an impending tragedy soon developed. An acrid smell of smoke began permeating the theater auditorium followed by the arrival of light smoke, all emanating from the basement area of an adjoining business, the Sunshine Corner Women's Apparel Shop. Within minutes, a basement fire was spreading quickly, threatening the theater itself and hundreds of attendees, mostly children, inside.

The Strand Theater, with a seating capacity of over one thousand in its main auditorium and balcony, was part of the Oppenheimer Building, a large business structure located on the southeast corner of Main and Oak Streets in the heart of Shenandoah's busy downtown business district. The four-story Oppenheimer Building, owned by ninety-year-old Morris Oppenheimer, also housed several additional businesses, apartments and professional offices. The building had a seventy-five-foot frontage along South Main Street and ran the length of the block eastward to Market Street.

Upon hearing reports of a fire, theater manager Max Abrams soon turned lights on in the auditorium and ordered the entire audience to evacuate the theater through the fire exits onto East Oak Street. Quickly but orderly, several hundred theater attendees, mostly children, were flooding onto Oak Street through all fire exits. The rapid onrush of air through multiple open fire doors helped spread the basement fire throughout the massive structure. Almost miraculously, all theater attendees and theater employees were successfully evacuated with no injuries or loss of life. A passing pedestrian, noticing the smoke, transmitted the fire alarm from Box 23, Main and Oak Streets at 1:32 p.m. The sounding of the municipal fire alarm summoned all five companies of the Shenandoah Fire Department. Arriving companies immediately knew they had a "major worker" on their hands.

Seeing the severity of the fire upon his arrival, Fire Chief Cornelius Reese established command and immediately called a second alarm, bringing all reserve fire apparatus and auxiliary personnel of the Shenandoah Fire Department to the scene. Responding first and second alarm apparatus included the Columbia No. 1's 1949 Seagrave pumper and 1921 American La France pumper, responding from only one block away. The Phoenix No. 2 and Polish American No. 4 companies both sent their 1954 Seagraves pumpers and 1941 Mack Type 45 pumpers to the scene. The Defender No. 3 responded in its 1939 White pumper, and the Rescue Hook & Ladder No. 1 set up its 1947 Seagraves tillered ladder on South Main Street onto the roof of the Oppenheimer Building. Multiple fire hydrants in the blocks surrounding the burning building were charged, and attack and supply lines, mostly two-and-a-half-inch hose, were established.

Despite valiant efforts by the volunteer firefighters to establish an interior attack on the fire, heavy, choking smoke soon enveloped not only the entire building itself but also a large section of the downtown business district, seriously hampering any offensive attempts to battle the blaze. Shenandoah firefighters placed multiple two-and-a-half-inch hose lines into service in a vain effort to control the fire. During the six-hour battle to control the blaze, eleven firefighters were injured; of these, nine firefighters were transported by Shenandoah ambulances to nearby Locust Mountain Hospital for smoke inhalation. At 4:20 p.m., the roof of the Oppenheimer Building gave way, and the magnitude of the fire became apparent. The fire began spreading east to Market Street and northward along South Main Street.

Fearing that an entire block of the business district might be lost to the inferno, Chief Reese made a general call for additional help from all neighboring communities and localities as far away as Pottsville, Minersville, Tamaqua, and Hazleton. Answering the plea for help were fire companies from Shenandoah Heights, William Penn, Lost Creek, Girardville,

Mahanoy City, Gilberton, Mahanoy Plane, Ringtown and Frackville. Soon, despite the bitter cold weather, several hundred firefighters were on scene, battling the stubborn blaze. Fire Chief Andy Hoke of the Pottsville Fire Department dispatched the Good Intent Fire Company with its 1958 Oren pumper and the West End Hose Company with its 1960 Seagrave ladder truck. Minersville Fire Chief George Ulmer sent the Rescue Company with its 1959 Ford Snorkel truck, the first of its kind in the county. Ironically, Minersville firefighters had demonstrated their new Ford Snorkel truck on the Oppenheimer Building several months earlier during a fire prevention program in Shenandoah as part of the Schuylkill County Volunteer Firefighters' Association Convention.

With several hundred volunteer firefighters on the scene and multiple ladder trucks and master stream hose lines in operation, Chief Reese finally began to gain headway on the blaze. A brick fire wall separated the Oppenheimer Building from additional businesses on South Main Street and fortuitously stopped the northern spread of the fire. Firefighters were

Fire originating in the Oppenheimer Building threatens the entire block on South Main Street in the Borough. Fire apparatus from Pottsville, including the Good Intent Fire Company Oren pumper and the West End Hose Company Seagrave aerial ladder truck, operate on scene that December day. Note the Bangor ladder with the tell-tale tormentor poles raised to the exposure building in the photo. *Glore collection.*

successful in gaining access to several buildings on South Market Street, the street directly behind the Oppenheimer Building, and stopped the eastward spread of the fire there. Shenandoah municipal water authority personnel later reported over one and a half million gallons of water were used through the hydrant system during firefighting operations. Six hours after the fire alarm sounded, Chief Reese finally declared the fire under control, and he began to release out-of-town fire companies from service.

The aftermath of this fire revealed the incredible destruction it reaped on the community and its popular business district. In addition to the loss of the Strand Theater, other businesses destroyed included O'Neill's Book Store, Goodman's Department Store, Zakarewicz Jewelry and Music Store, the Veterans of Foreign Wars Post Home and the Sunshine Corner Woman's Shop, where the fire reportedly began. Thankfully, no loss of life occurred at this fire. Additionally, eleven volunteer firefighters and one resident were treated at the Locust Mountain Hospital. The resident, eighty-one-year-old Sadie Hares, was carried from her burning apartment by firefighters and transported by ambulance to the hospital. Insurance losses were estimated between $1 and $1.5 million. State police and local investigators never officially determined the cause of this fire, although it was believed that plumbers using torches to thaw frozen pipes in the basement of the Sunshine Corner Woman's Shop may have started the blaze. Sadly, *Pinocchio in Outer Space* was never shown again, as the Strand Theater and the other businesses destroyed by the fire were not rebuilt. Thus ended an important and tragic chapter of Shenandoah history.

12

BEWARE THE IDES OF MARCH

MARCH 28, 1954

The month of March 1954 proved to be a challenging time for members of the Coaldale Volunteer Fire Company No. 1. The fire company, organized in 1906, protected an eastern Schuylkill County borough of over five thousand people in 1954. A major fire on March 15 of that year destroyed the Lankalis Tavern and apartments and damaged several residences on East High Street, a fire that at one point threatened the entire block. That fire also challenged the resources of the Coaldale Volunteer Fire Company and required the help of the American Fire Company No. 1 of Lansford to bring under control. Less than two weeks later, on Sunday, March 28, another disastrous fire would severely damage a prominent business in the community, Soberick's Home and Auto Supply along Route 209 (Water Street) in Coaldale. Also destroyed in the blaze was the adjoining apartment of business owner George Soberick. Only valiant efforts by firefighters saved several adjacent properties from destruction.

Two employees of the business, Harry McDonald and Bernard Stone, discovered the fire at 6:20 p.m., about the same time that George Soberick and his brother-in-law, Joseph Modrick of Lansford, started to investigate the smell of smoke. Upon the discovery of the fire, George's son, Jack, who had been near the garage area, raced to First and Water Streets and transmitted the fire alarm from Box 12. McDonald and Stone connected a garden hose and started to battle the flames, pending the arrival of borough firefighters. They were soon joined by Soberick and Modrick in a vain early attempt to control the fire.

Above: The American Fire Company of Lansford operates at the Soberick's fire in Coaldale in 1954 with the company's state-of-the-art 1951 GMC/Approved rescue truck with its light tower raised. *Kevin Soberick Collection.*

Opposite: These smoke eaters advance a hose line over a ground ladder at the Soberick's fire. *Kevin Soberick Collection.*

The sounding of the municipal fire alarm brought a full and quick response from the Coaldale Volunteer Fire Company No. 1 from their quarters on Third Street. Coaldale fire apparatus responding included their 1941 Hahn city service truck and 1928 Seagrave pumper. Coaldale Fire Chief Andrew Mikolay took command and, seeing the severity of the blaze, immediately ordered several large two-and-a-half-inch hose lines to be placed into service. With deposits of oil, grease and a large supply of tires within the building, the fire soon turned into a raging inferno. After twenty minutes and with several large hose lines having no effect on the fire, Chief Mikolay again made a call for help at 6:55 p.m. to the American Fire Company No. 1 of Lansford.

Realizing the potential danger of a gasoline explosion, George Soberick quickly cut the electrical switches leading to his gas pumps. With six thousand gallons of highly flammable gasoline in his tanks, Soberick wanted to avert a possible catastrophe. Fire Chief Norman Tippett of Lansford soon arrived

on scene and assisted Chief Mikolay in directing firefighting operations in what eventually became an eight-hour battle. Fire apparatus arriving from Lansford included a 1951 GMC rescue truck, a 1954 Pirsch aerial ladder truck and a 1947 Ahrens-Fox piston pumper. Additionally, the South Ward Fire Company of Tamaqua sent manpower and gas masks to the scene to assist in the firefighting efforts. Their trucks remained "on stand-by" in Tamaqua should additional help be needed.

Upon learning of the fire, Coaldale Police Officer Ronald Murphy quickly arrived on the scene and executed a heroic rescue. Battling both intense fire and smoke, Officer Murphy made a dramatic dash into the burning building and retrieved George Soberick's filing cabinet. Soberick described the filing cabinet as invaluable to the business. In the early stages of the blaze, both McDonald and Stone also ran back into the fire building and saved Soberick's cash register as well as a few new bicycles and additional inventory. Everything else in the store was described by Soberick as a total loss, a loss of inventory that Soberick estimated at $100,000.

As soon as Lansford's volunteers arrived at the fire scene, Chief Tibbett ordered the big Ahrens-Fox piston pumper onto a hydrant to supply several additional two-and-a-half-inch hose lines to the blaze. Furthermore, Chief

Firefighters work over ground ladders to access the roof of Soberick's business. *Kevin Soberick Collection.*

The "Firestone" tires advertising sign is clearly visible as smoke pushes from the overhead door leading to the auto service bay. *Kevin Soberick Collection.*

Tibbett had Lansford's GMC rescue truck illuminate the entire fire scene with its large floodlights. The height of the flames, intensity of the smoke and the eerie glow in the sky served to attract hundreds of spectators to that location. Chief Mikolay and Officer Murphy ordered Coaldale Auxiliary Fire Police to detour traffic off busy Route 209 and maintain crowd control. Several scary moments frightened both firefighters and spectators alike as three separate explosions rocked the burning building and sent firefighters scurrying. Chief Mikolay attributed the explosions to drums of antifreeze exploding inside the building.

During the intense, multi-hour fight to control the blaze, two firefighters were overcome by the heavy smoke condition and required medical treatment. Simon Stafiniak, a member of the Coaldale Volunteer Fire Company, while fighting the fire from a roof, collapsed on scene and was removed from the roof on a litter. Stafiniak was taken to the Lansford rescue truck, where oxygen was administered by Dr. Marvin Evans of Lansford. Stafiniak, accompanied by Dr. Evans, was then placed in the Coaldale Community Ambulance and transported to Coaldale State Hospital, where he was admitted. Dr. Evans returned to the fire scene, where his services were again needed. Lansford Fire Chief Norman Tippett also succumbed to the smoke.

As flames ravage the Soberick building, men salvage a filing cabinet in order to preserve business records. *Kevin Soberick Collection.*

He, too, was taken to the Lansford rescue truck and administered oxygen. Tibbett responded to the oxygen treatment by Dr. Evans and returned to help Chief Mikolay direct firefighting efforts.

After an eight-hour battle, the fire was finally declared out about 2:00 a.m. Firefighters from Lansford gathered their equipment and headed back to town. Coaldale firefighters and fire police remained on the scene throughout the night, wetting down hotspots and preventing possible looting. The massive destruction of the fire prevented investigators from learning the cause of the blaze. George Soberick and his family relocated temporarily with the Modrick family in Lansford. Estimates of the total loss of the buildings and inventory exceeded $200,000, a sum that was only partially covered by insurance. George Soberick made the decision to rebuild his business at the same location. Within a year of the disastrous fire, Soberick's Home and Auto Supply Store was back in business, a successful business that continued for several decades and was later operated by George Soberick's son, Jack Soberick.

13

SO THAT OTHERS MAY LIVE

APRIL 27, 1982

I t was a rainy and somewhat dreary Tuesday evening as the five friends cruised around southern Schuylkill County in the 1973 Plymouth Cuda. It was around 11:00 p.m. The rural roads were dark save for the lights of the homes in the area. Two seventeen-year-old young men were riding in the front seats while another seventeen-year-old young man, an eighteen-year-old young man and a nineteen-year-old young woman were in the back seats.

After tooling around the area most of the evening, the driver stopped the car in McKeansburg in East Brunswick Township. The eighteen-year-old backseat passenger and the seventeen-year-old front seat passenger switched positions. The driver took off east on State Route 895 at a very high rate of speed. The young woman in the back seat asked the driver why he was driving so fast. With that, the driver slammed on the brakes. With the rainy conditions and the wet roadway, all friction was lost between the tires and the road surface.

Screams filled the car as it slid sideways almost one hundred feet along the roadway. It slammed broadside into a utility pole, which caused the car to be split in half and the utility pole to the sheared off approximately ten feet off the ground. The youthful friends crumpled into each other. It was bad...very bad.

Help was summoned immediately. The Community Fire Company of New Ringgold and the Friendship Fire Company of Orwigsburg responded along with ambulances from Orwigsburg, New Ringgold and Penn-Mahoning.

The Plymouth Cuda was severed when it struck the utility pole, causing devastating injuries to the occupants of the vehicle. *Schuylkill County Historical Society.*

As emergency personnel arrived, the severity of the crash was obvious. It was also obvious that some of the occupants would need to be extricated from the vehicle. Via the Southern Schuylkill Mutual Aid dispatch center in Schuylkill Haven, the Rainbow Hose Company of Schuylkill Haven was summoned for the HURST hydraulic rescue tools carried on the company's 1958 International/1980 Swab heavy rescue truck, Rescue 727.

Rainbow arrived on scene as extrication efforts were underway. Some of the victims that were less severely injured were transported to local hospitals. The driver of the car was killed. It was clear to the emergency medical technicians and rescue firefighters on scene that the front seat passenger was critically injured. He was suffering from obvious head injuries, a fractured pelvis and hypovolemic shock. He would need surgical intervention at a trauma center as quickly as possible. The rescue chief made the call: The victim would be flown from the scene.

The Allentown and Sacred Heart Hospital (ASH) started a helicopter medical flight program on May 6, 1981, known as Med-Evac. These were inter-facility flights only. On April 8, 1982, the program began landing at incident scenes to provide rapid transportation of critical patients and accident victims. In Vietnam in 1963, the term "dust off" was coined, which referred to medical evacuation missions via helicopter. On that Tuesday evening in late April, it would be only the fourth time that the medical helicopter would be used to transport a victim from an incident scene. The helicopter used by ASH was leased from the Keystone Helicopter Corporation of West Chester, Pennsylvania. That firm also supplied the pilots.

At 10:36 p.m., the twenty-five-year-old on-duty pilot had received a weather briefing. At 11:12 p.m., a request for the Med-Evac helicopter to respond for the victim of an automobile accident in Schuylkill County was received. In ten minutes, the Messerschmitt-Bölkow-Blohm BO-105C helicopter was in the air with a thirty-five-year-old flight nurse as well as a twenty-four-year-old flight medic. The helicopter, with its Nightsun searchlight activated, landed safely in rainy and breezy conditions at 11:43 p.m. in a field near the intersection of State Routes 443 and 895.

Medical personnel from the helicopter met emergency personnel from the scene who had transported the victim to the landing zone. This was going to be a "hot load"—the helicopter's engines would be running and the rotors turning while the patient was loaded. With the patient loaded, the helicopter was cleared for takeoff. With its searchlight blazing, it departed toward the southeast. Less than a minute after takeoff and approximately five hundred yards from the landing zone south of Route 895, the helicopter hit rising terrain in a steep nose-down attitude and in a right bank. Slamming into the

Emergency personnel carry the crucially injured male occupant of the vehicle to the waiting helicopter. The pilot is in the left of the photo near the rear of the aircraft. *Schuylkill County Historical Society.*

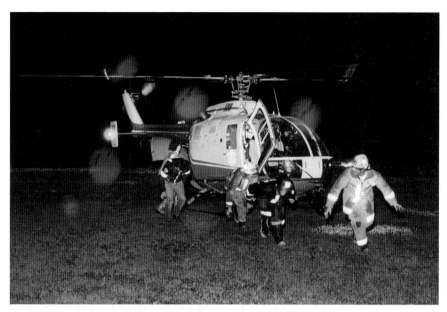

Top: The "hot load" completed, emergency personnel make their way from the helicopter as it prepares for departure. *Schuylkill County Historical Society*.

Bottom: The remains of the helicopter continue to burn after it had slammed into a field not long after takeoff. The aircrew gave their lives in the crash attempting to save another. *Schuylkill County Historical Society*.

Opposite: Terribly poignant reminder of the sacrifice made by the aircrew that night—the pilot's boot resting not far from the crash site. *Schuylkill County Historical Society*.

The *Pottsville Republican* newspaper headlines told the tale of the tragic accident involving the medial helicopter in McKeansburg in April 1982. *Glore collection.*

Nightmare at McKeansburg

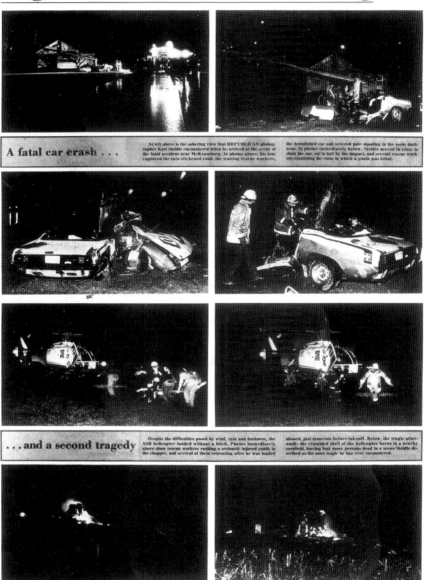

The *Pottsville Republican* photographer Kurt Steidle was at the scene when the crash occurred, and he captured these dramatic images.

earth, the aircraft erupted in a fireball in a cornfield. Parts of the helicopter were scattered over a forty-yard area on top of the hilly field: medical supplies, chunks of the tail and engine and, tragically, the remains of those on board. The time was 11:55 p.m.

Onlookers were stunned and horrified. As they raced to the scene as quickly as possible, the scope of the tragedy became immediately apparent. The aircrew had given their lives in an attempt to save the life of another.

The State Bureau of Aviation investigator arrived on the scene at 4:00 a.m. He was quickly followed by the Pennsylvania State Police Aviation Division as well as National Transportation Safety Board (NTSB) investigators who responded form JFK Airport in New York City.

As the investigation was underway, over five hundred people attended a memorial service for the flight crew on May 1, 1982. A memorial fund was also established for the flight crew and their families with local organizations taking the lead: the Little Schuylkill Lions Club, the International Order of Odd Fellows and the Community Fire Company of New Ringgold.

In 1984, the NTSB released its final report on the crash. "Pilot error" was largely the summation of the report, resulting in an uncontrolled descent, which then concluded in an in-flight collision with the terrain. With no visual reference on the ground and the pilot unable to see the horizon, spatial disorientation was found to be a critical problem. Other factors such as the dark of night, the low ceiling, rain and the hilly terrain were also cited. It was also noted that the pilot had limited experience in adverse weather and lacked sufficient instrument panel experience for the weather conditions. The twenty-five-year-old pilot had 1,913 hours of flight experience but only 75 hours in that particular type of helicopter.

Lawsuits were initiated as a result of the crash. In March 1989, a Philadelphia jury awarded the estate of the flight nurse who had been on board the aircraft $1.4 million. In 1990, the estate of the vehicle accident victim who was on board the helicopter was awarded a $1.2 million settlement, which was split between the helicopter manufacturer, the vendor who supplied the helicopter to ASH and the driver of the automobile involved in the accident.

This was an event that proved to be horrific for all involved. The incident was early in the medical helicopter program in the region and, as with all such tragic events such as this, resulted in protocol changes for these types of flights. While investigations are certainly warranted in these instances, their findings in no way detract from the efforts of the flight crew who chose service over self.

14

THE FIREWORKS CONTINUED

JULY 5, 1990

While walking from his Frackville home to work this hot July morning, Mike Metchock pondered what an easy day he had in store. The plant where he worked, Saint Jude Polymer on South Broad Mountain Avenue, was still officially closed for the July 4 holiday. All Mike had to do was work a few hours with two fellow workers to conduct a plant test, and then it was a jaunt home for the rest of the weekend. Little did Mike consider that it would be his last day of work at St. Jude Polymer. Soon after arriving for work at 6:15 a.m., one of his fellow workers, the plant janitor, discovered a smoky haze in the southwest corner of the block-long building. When the workers opened the doors of the loading dock, they were met by a fire, fed by a large volume of cardboard boxes, which was spreading rapidly toward the wooden roof of the structure. Confronted with a large volume of flames and smoke, Mike Metchock, a member of Frackville's Good Will Hose Company No. 1, instinctively ran to nearby Fire Alarm Box 24, Arch and South Broad Mountain Avenues and "hooked the box!"

In 1977, the St. Jude Polymer Corporation began recycling polyester scrap and polyethylene terephthalate (PET) containers—two-liter soda bottles. The company came to handle over fifteen million tons of scrap per year. In 1983, the company purchased a forty-five-thousand-square-foot building to handle much of their recycling business in the 300 block of South Broad Mountain Avenue in Frackville, a mostly residential neighborhood. The company's fire insurance rates were quite high due to the recycling processes taking place within the large building with its wooden roof. The building was what the new company could afford at the time. In 1987, St. Jude Polymer began a major expansion and purchased the former Metropolitan Mirror and Glass plant in the Frackville Industrial Park. At eighty-four thousand square feet, this building was nearly double the size of the South Broad Mountain Avenue facility. The company had been looking for ways to expand production due to the demand for the plastic pellets produced.

The sounding of the Frackville Municipal Fire Alarm brought a quick response of firefighters from the Good Will, located only a few blocks away, as well as the Altamont Fire Company, close by in West Mahanoy Township, and the Friendship of Englewood, located nearby in Butler Township. Calls soon began flooding the Schuylkill County Communications Center as well, then still located in the basement of the Schuylkill County Court House. Dispatcher Ande Ebling arrived a few minutes early for the start of his day shift. He relieved the night shift dispatchers as the initial call for the fire came in. His partner, Will Heffner, also arrived, and in Ande's words, "It was nothing but tones the rest of the day!"

Arriving firefighters were soon confronted with a massive wall of fire from the almost block-long building. The fire had already spread to the roof, self-vented and, with the prevailing wind, was whipping toward the private homes to the east in the 300 block of South Broad Mountain Avenue. First on scene was Frackville Good Will's 1974 American La France one-hundred-foot quint ladder truck, initially positioned on the southwest corner of the blazing structure. Realizing the severity of exposed residential homes on South Broad Mountain Avenue, the firefighting team was quick to reposition the ladder truck to the northeast corner where a master stream ladder pipe and a deluge gun were set up. Good Will's 1980 Hahn pumper established a water supply, and the company's Ford rescue truck was utilized as a command post at the corner of Broad Mountain Avenue and Arch Streets. The Friendship of Englewood arrived with their 1972 Mack pumper and operated a master stream on the northwest corner. Altamont's 1984 Ford/Hahn pumper established several master streams in the southwest corner. The Frackville Police assisted with the immediate evacuation of exposed homes along South Broad Mountain Avenue.

Frackville Fire Chief Orval Palsgrove established command at Broad Mountain Avenue and Arch Streets and, realizing the magnitude of the fire that he and "his troops" were facing, began to summon mutual aid. Palsgrove's initial request was for ladder trucks; Saint Clair's Rescue company soon responded with its 1971 Ford/Howe sixty-five-foot quint followed by the Washington Hook & Ladder of Mahanoy City with its

Flames spread rapidly through the large recycling facility, completely destroying the plant. *Schuylkill County Historical Society.*

1973 American La France one-hundred-foot aerial ladder, both of which were immediately pressed into service. Chief Palsgrove also requested companies with large diameter hose (LDH). In response to this request, the City of Pottsville sent the Humane with its 1980 Seagrave 1250-GPM pumper and the American Hose, with its 1984 American La France 1500-GPM pumper, both with several thousand feet of LDH. Also dispatched early to the incident were the Citizens of Mahanoy City with their 1975 Mack 1000-GPM pumper and the Good Will of Port Carbon with its 1987 Pirsch 1500-GPM pumper. These two companies were ordered to protect the nearby homes exposed to the fire and to initiate fire attack in those properties already burning.

The homes exposed to the fire were located across the street from St. Jude Polymer along South Broad Mountain Avenue. Some of these two-and-a-half-story wood-frame duplex homes were receiving severe radiant heat and even direct flame impingement. Several of these homes ignited, some of which became serious fires. Firefighters focused their efforts on protecting these homes. Two homes, 339 and 341 South Broad Mountain Avenue, were severely damaged, and fifteen homes in total received damage from this blaze. As PPL transformers along the Broad Mountain Avenue side failed, electrical service was cut to approximately two thousand customers in the Frackville, Gilberton, Maizeville, Mahanoy Plane and Girardville areas until

9:00 a.m. Power was then restored, and the service interruption was isolated to those properties in the immediate area of the fire building.

Fire officials soon realized early in the incident that the byproducts of the burning plastic materials could well pose a danger to residents. The evacuation was expanded to include fifty homes, which totaled approximately two hundred residents. Lending support to the command staff was Schuylkill County Emergency Management Agency and its coordinator, Art Kaplan. The decision was made to have the Pennsylvania Department of Environmental Protection (DEP) respond to the scene with a mobile laboratory and perform air monitoring. Command staff also decided that foam should be used to fight the fire remaining in the St. Jude building. By this time, much of the roof had burned away and portions of the block walls of the building had collapsed. Additionally, Incident Commander Orv Palsgrove was advised by his municipal water authority that the large flow from the municipal hydrants could not be sustained indefinitely without creating an emergency water situation.

Locating foam supplies and water tankers, in addition to dispatching additional fire apparatus for fighting the fire, made the basement communications center an extremely busy place. Lacking the computer help today, essentially, dispatchers Ande Ebling and Will Heffner, both county firefighters, used their extensive knowledge of Schuylkill County's fire service resources and those of surrounding counties to fulfill the incident commander's requests. Tankers came from both the northern and southern areas of the county. Foam came from throughout the county as well. In addition, the dispatchers knew of foam task forces in both Berks and Luzerne Counties and requested their services. Berks companies responding included Hamburg, Leesport and Good Will of Hyde Park (Muhlenberg Township). Luzerne companies answering the call included West Hazleton, Freeland, Harwood, Hazle Township and Weatherly. Furthermore, dispatchers also requested a foam unit from Fort Indiantown Gap in Lebanon County. With all dispatching and fireground communication being done on the 46.50 radio frequency, interruptions did occur. Fortunately, no other serious incidents developed that day, and county police departments, hearing the volume of emergency traffic on the radio, kept their radio communications and telephone calls to a minimum.

By 2:30 p.m., over eight hours since the alarm sounded, the fire was sufficiently quelled to allow heavy equipment from Fidler Brothers Construction, Pottsville, to clear paths into the building, dig out hotspots and separate some of the burning debris. In all, 3000 gallons of foam was used on the fire at an approximate cost (1990 dollars) of $35,000. In addition, water authority officials estimated approximately 1 million gallons of water was used in fighting the fire. Of that total, 260,000 thousand gallons of water were transported to the scene by fire department tankers. A tanker fill site was initially established at the Schuylkill Mall but was later relocated to the Schuylkill County Fire Training Grounds on the Morea Road.

With the fire finally extinguished, the incident remained open, as it was not until Monday, July 9, that the remaining evacuated residents were given approval to return to their homes. DEP's analysis had then indicated that no chemical hazards remained. A community meeting later that day resulted in Fire Chief Orval Palsgrove and Emergency Management Coordinator Arthur Kaplan being virtually bombarded with questions from concerned residents. Of particular concern were elevated levels of polyvinyl chloride—a byproduct of the burning plastic.

Damage estimates of the fire totaled $2 million. Thirty-five employees of the South Broad Mountain Avenue plant were out of work. Some of those employees were relocated to the company's other plant in the Frackville Industrial Park while other employees were laid off. In addition, several residents of South Broad Mountain Avenue were displaced until repairs to their damaged homes could be completed. The cause of the fire was arson. In terms of sheer commitment of firefighting resources, the Saint Jude Polymer fire was certainly one of the largest fires in Schuylkill County history.

15

HEARTBREAK HOTEL

DECEMBER 27, 1992

Fred Herb and Bill Jones, both of Tamaqua, were working the early morning shift at the Hess Gas Station in downtown Tamaqua. While cleaning a customer's windshield and pumping gas, Jones noticed smoke pouring from the Tamaqua Hotel across the street at 8 West Broad Street. While Jones was reporting the fire on his cellphone, Herb ran to nearby Box 32, Broad and Centre Streets, and pulled the hook. The sounding of the municipal fire alarm and the blaring of fire pagers provided a rude and cruel awakening for many Tamaqua firefighters and residents on a cloudy, cold Sunday morning at eight o'clock on December 27, 1992. The cheerfulness of the Christmas season came to an abrupt ending as smoke soon engulfed the downtown area, and fire began enveloping the second and third floors of the building, home to about twenty Tamaqua residents. Unknown to arriving firefighters, the fire would claim a life of one of these residents. Tamaqua companies responding to the general alarm were American Hose, Citizens, East End and South Ward Fire Companies.

Tragedy had previously struck this location, then known as the Keller Hotel, twenty-six years earlier. On Sunday, May 1, 1966, firefighters responding to Box 32 found heavy fire conditions spreading up the interior stairwell to the upper floors. Tamaqua Fire Chief Paul Behr ordered ground ladders extended to all exterior windows and hose lines advanced into the hotel to knock down the fire. In the early stages of the 1966 fire, multiple rescues were conducted by ground ladders. A total of fifteen occupants were

Smoke pours from the Tamaqua Hotel on that bitterly cold December morning. *Glore collection.*

rescued in this manner. After a three-hour battle, Chief Behr placed the fire under control. Sadly, however, two occupants perished in the 1966 blaze, seventy-year-old Kenneth Spayd and sixty-eight-year-old John Kastrava. Also, a firefighter, James Kunkel, age thirty-two, and a resident, seventy-three-year-old Benjamin Schlosser, were both treated at Coaldale Hospital for injuries.

Sandra Kopac, aged thirty-two, rented a room on the second floor of the Tamaqua Hotel. Sandra and several of her friends would often meet at the bar and grille of the hotel, located on the first floor. Plans were already being advanced for a New Year's Eve reunion between Sandra and several of these friends, all of whom first met at Tamaqua Hotel bar and grille. According to Sandra's boyfriend, forty-one-year-old Joseph Clausis, Sandra heard smoke alarms sounding and investigated immediately. Upon seeing smoke conditions in a nearby hallway bathroom, Sandra awakened her boyfriend and began knocking on hotel doors to rouse the guests. An attempt was also made to put out the fire with a portable fire extinguisher. The boyfriend pleaded with Sandra to exit the building. She started leaving the hotel but suddenly turned around and rushed to the third floor to make sure all those residents there had evacuated. This would be the last time Joseph Clausis saw her alive.

Arriving Tamaqua firefighters were confronted with a daunting task: how to rescue remaining hotel guests under rapidly deteriorating conditions and how to bring this major fire under control. Many older firefighters harbored vivid memories of the almost miraculous rescue efforts that occurred in the same building in the 1966 fire. Among the earliest arriving first responders were Police Officer Edward Carroll and Police Detective George Woodward, both of whom were on duty just two blocks away. Their attempts to enter the hotel were quickly thwarted, however, due to heavy fire conditions. Fire Chief Art Connely, upon arrival, immediately took command and ordered ladders raised and multiple hose lines charged. At this point, flames had spread throughout interior stairwells up to the fourth floor of the hotel. Adjoining the property to the west was the M&S Hardware Store, a well-established business in the community and a survivor of the 1966 fire, primarily due to an existing fire wall. Would this fire wall again stop the westward spread of the blaze? A quick survey of hotel residents soon revealed that one person remained missing, Sandra Kopac.

Chief Connely ordered Tamaqua firefighters into the hardware store to determine if the fire had spread into that building. Firefighters searching the

Top: Pumpers from the American Hose Company and the Citizens Fire Company, both of Tamaqua, supply hose lines to battle the blaze. *Glore collection.*

Bottom: Tamaqua Fire Department's 1978 American LaFrance one-hundred-foot aerial ladder truck—Ladder 1—operates at the Tamaqua Hotel Fire. *Glore collection.*

Looking over the cab of the American Hose Company's 1981 Ford/Darley pumper, one can see powerful hose streams being directed into the upper floors of the Tamaqua Hotel. *Glore collection.*

hardware store were pleased with the assortment of tools readily available on the shelves. Using these tools, firefighters attempted to breach the hardware store wall and enter the third floor of the hotel with a hose line. Untenable fire conditions in the building prevented them from any advancement. Chief Connely remained concerned about this exposure as a fire spread into the hardware store could easily transition to a "block burner." Hotel owners Frederick and Catharine Stewart of Mount Pocono were both vacationing in Florida at the time of the fire. Hotel manager Eugene Moerder also was not present at that time.

Considering the enormity of the task before him and with firefighters working in subfreezing temperatures, Chief Connely immediately sought mutual aid from surrounding communities. The American Fire Company of Lansford responded with their seventy-five-foot ladder truck, a 1992 E-One. Supplying pumpers and additional manpower were the Hometown Fire Company with their 1977 Pierce/Hendrickson and New England Fire Company in their 1992 Ford/Darley. Ryan Township Fire Company was placed on standby for additional support or to handle other fire calls in the community. Chief Connely also sought EMS assistance; assisting the

A view looking east on West Broad Street with the American Fire Company of Lansford operating the company's seventy-five-foot E-One aerial ladder truck. *Glore collection.*

Tamaqua Community Ambulance Squad were medical units from Ryan Township, Lansford and Schuylkill Township. Also responding were the Tamaqua Rescue Squad and the Tamaqua Salvation Army.

As fire completely engulfed the interior of the Tamaqua Hotel, a defensive operation was established by the chief. Multiple hose lines were placed in service on the roof of the M&S Hardware Store to help prevent a westward spread of the flames. Additional master streams flooded the hotel from the front, rear and east side. Due to the valiant efforts of Tamaqua firefighters, no fire damage occurred in the hardware store, although some smoke and water damage occurred. The M&S fire wall held again. After a four-hour defensive battle with numerous master streams in operation, Chief Connely declared the fire under control about noon. With temperatures remaining below freezing throughout the day, ice coated everything and everyone. The task remaining was no less daunting: where was Sandra Kopac?

With the fire well under control, early attempts to reenter the hotel to search for Sandra Kopac were made. However, various sections of the roof and interior had collapsed into the building, and the structural stability of the hotel was seriously compromised. Firefighters labored well into the night removing mounds of frozen debris in their efforts to locate Kopac's body, but their progress was painfully slow. Due to increased concerns for the structural integrity of the building, Chief Connely halted firefighters' efforts, and borough officials requested the services of the Northeast Search and Rescue Team. Using their specialty-trained dogs, Northeast teams made several attempts to locate Kopac's body, but these attempts also proved unsuccessful. A special call was then made to the Rescue Hook and Ladder Company of Minersville for use of their 1963 Ford/Pitman Snorkel truck and recently purchased 1977 Seagrave/LTI eighty-five-foot ladder tower. While both trucks provided a stable platform for searchers to gain access to the third floor, these efforts also proved in vain.

Sandra Kopac's body was finally discovered on the stairway between the second and third floor of the hotel by workers of the Lycoming and Excavating Company on Thursday afternoon, December 31, four days after the fire occurred. Using dental records, Kopac's body was positively identified by Schuylkill County deputy coroner Jean Linkhorst. Noting what appeared to be several sources of origin of the fire, State Police fire marshal Joseph Woziak, working with borough police and fire officials, determined that this fire was deliberately set and ruled it as an arson/homicide. Who set this deadly fire? The case remains as an open investigation with the Pennsylvania State Police to this day.

16

A MUSICAL TRAGEDY

FEBRUARY 2, 1991

Members of the Falcons' Drill Team of Salisbury High School in Lehigh County, Pennsylvania, were brimming with confidence and anticipation on that early February morning in 1991. That day would commence the first of more than a dozen competitions against high school drill teams across the state of Pennsylvania. Months of practice and hard work for the Falcons would hopefully produce a coveted team trophy for their school. The February 2 competition was scheduled to begin sharply at 10:00 a.m. at Upper Dauphin High School in Elizabethville with twenty-six high schools competing.

The route to Upper Dauphin High School passed directly through the mountains of western Schuylkill County along U.S. Route 209, an old two-lane road that traversed the entire Schuylkill County from east to west. Could the late arrival of the team's charter bus that morning at Salisbury High School have been a bad portent of things to come? The charter bus, a Belgium-made Van Hool bus, came from the Leonard Lines Bus Company of nearby Whitehall and was driven by veteran driver John Snyder, age sixty-two. As drill team members, from grades six to 12, and their chaperones filled the bus to its forty-six-passenger capacity, an additional car caravan of parents and friends also departed to Elizabethville, a destination the drill team bus would never achieve.

At approximately 10:05 a.m. on Route 209, while still twenty minutes from the competition, the drill team bus suddenly skidded sharply to the left, crashed through guard rails and plunged 150 feet down a steep embankment on Keffers' Mountain. Tall trees on the mountainside prevented the bus from overturning and descending even farther. Several passengers were propelled through the windshield of the bus, and all forty-six passengers were injured, some seriously and one fatally. The accident occurred approximately one mile west of the village of Joliett in Porter Township. Within minutes, the Schuylkill County 911 Center was flooded with calls reporting the accident and seeking identification of its occupants.

POTTSVILLE *touching your life every day* REPUBLICAN

Schuylkill County's Newspaper ▷ SINCE 1884 ◁ A Pulitzer Prize Winner

VOL. CCXIV — NO. 82   POTTSVILLE, PA. MONDAY, FEBRUARY 4, 1991   35¢ A SINGLE COPY

Troopers seek cause of bus crash

Was driver distracted, speeding?
One killed, 45 injured in plunge

By Erica Franklin
The REPUBLICAN

JOLIETT — State police this morning were still trying to determine why a chartered bus carrying a Lehigh Valley drill team pitched 150 feet over the side of Keffers Mountain on Route 209 a mile west of here at 10:05 a.m. Saturday.

A chaperone died in the crash, two team members were flown to Geisinger and Hershey medical centers, three others were taken to a Harrisburg hospital, and 46 — including the bus driver — were treated at the two Pottsville hospitals.

The students were from the Salisbury Area School District in Salisbury Township, south of Allentown, and were en route to a drill-team competition at Upper Dauphin High School, Elizabethville.

There were 46 people on the bus.

Saturday, troopers and rescue workers at the scene were speculating that ice on the road or a blown tire may have caused the driver, John W. Snyder Sr., 62, of Bethlehem, to lose control of the bus, although those explanations appeared to be discounted today.

Reached by phone this morning, Trooper James Wixted, Schuylkill Haven, the investigator, said another scenario is being explored: That Snyder leaned over to pick up a dropped thermos bottle just before the crash.

"We interviewed him yesterday and will be interviewing other people on the bus today," Wixted said. "We should have some conclusions by the end of the week."

Another scenario, speeding, will be looked into today as police inspect skid marks on the pavement and measure the grade, and Wixted. Asked if the bus driver, due at 7 a.m., had not arrived to pick up the students until 9, Clarence J. Jones, Salisbury Area assistant superintendent, would only say the schools is "preparing a report" on that matter.

The dead man was identified as Robert Growcott, 37, of

903 Benton St., Allentown, one of three chaperones on the trip. According to one report, he was the fiance of the drill team instructor, Donna Temlin.

Growcott was thrown to the front of the bus and through the windshield. He suffered massive head injuries, investigators said.

Two to five other passengers — the ones injured most severely — may have been flung 10 to 15 feet from the bus, according to rescue workers and students.

Only two people not thrown from the bus suffered seri-

(Please turn to page 8)

Ray Sikora/The REPUBLICAN

The bus driver, John W. Snyder Sr., 62, is lifted over guardrail on his way to Pottsville Hospital.

Crash terrifies parents, 2 teens

Allentown family recalls fright

By Matt Assad
The REPUBLICAN

Paulette Tretter's heart sank to her stomach when an emergency worker told her, "One male has been killed."

The mother knew her son Timothy was one of only four males on the bus that plunged through a Route 209 guiderail and vaulted 150 feet over a hillside near Joliett.

"I died a little when I heard that," she said Sunday. "I thought my Timothy was killed."

Timothy, 17, did not die when a charter bus carrying the Salisbury Area School District drill team and

Tragedy on wheels

- Gloom pervades accident scene.
- Pottsville's hospitals handle crisis.
- Complete list of injured.
- **Details, more photos, Pages 5, 8**

chaperones — 46 people in all — plunged down a steep hill.

Neither did his sister, Nichole, 16. But as the two teen-agers sat trapped in the bus, Paulette and George Tret-

(Please turn to page 6)

Up front

Hills company files for bankruptcy

Hills Department Stores Inc. filed for bankruptcy relief under Chapter 11 of the federal Bankruptcy Code, but the company's president said today that "business as usual" will continue at all Hills

Andy Matsko/The REPUBLICAN

The Leonard Lines' chartered bus is pulled back onto Route 209 near Joliett about 5 p.m. Saturday.

The *Pottsville Republican* front page following the tragic bus accident in February 1991.

Quickly realizing the severity of the incident, 911 dispatchers summoned multiple medical, rescue and fire units from western Schuylkill County and northern Dauphin County. Medical helicopters from both Geisinger and Hershey Medical Centers were also requested. Ambulances from Tremont, Pine Grove, Tower City, Lykens, Hegins and Williamstown were soon en route to the scene. Fire and Rescue units from Porter Township, Tower City and Tremont also responded. The first arriving Porter Township unit was the Reinerton Fire Company with Fire Chief Russ Good assuming command. Confronted with forty-six injured passengers, some seriously, a command decision was quickly made to establish a triage center at the nearby Joliett Fire Station and to have Joliett firefighters set up a landing zone for the incoming medical helicopters.

Rescuers descended the steep embankment and set up ropes, backboards and Stokes baskets to remove victims from the bus and move them to the triage area. They were assisted by numerous passersby who stopped to render aid. The most seriously injured were transported by helicopter to both Hershey Medical Center and Geisinger Medical Center. Following triage, ambulances and a school bus carried the less seriously injured to three hospitals: Polyclinic Medical Center in Harrisburg, Pottsville Hospital and the Good Samaritan Hospital, also in Pottsville. Both Pottsville hospitals were put on emergency alert soon after the accident occurred, and extra staff members, doctors and nurses were called in to assist. One bus chaperone, Robert Growcott, age thirty-seven, of Allentown, was propelled through the bus windshield and suffered fatal massive head injuries. He was pronounced dead at the scene. The driver, John Snyder, also incurred serious injuries and was admitted to Pottsville Hospital. Snyder survived the accident. Rescuers described the injured students on the bus as remaining very calm during the rescue operation. The last injured patient was removed to the triage center one hour and twenty-two minutes after the incident began.

Salisbury Township parents following behind the bus were detoured away from the accident scene as police soon closed Route 209 to all but emergency traffic. After learning that the bus was from a Whitehall company, many parents returned to the accident scene and to the triage center in a frantic attempt to learn the identities of the injured. Parents likewise made multiple calls to the hospitals for additional information. After hearing of the accident, Upper Dauphin High School principal Dermot M. Garrett quickly departed the drill competition at his school and arrived at the Joliett Fire Station triage center. He, too, wanted to learn the names of the injured and hospitals they were transported to. Garrett had the unenviable task of notifying the Salisbury Township parents who had arrived earlier at the high school for the competition.

By 11:30 a.m., all but a few emergency responders remained on scene. Tow trucks from Motter's Garage in Pine Grove worked over four hours to retrieve the heavily damaged bus from its perilous position over the embankment. Pennsylvania State Police investigated the accident but never fully determined the cause of it. One leading consideration was driver distraction, as it was reported that the bus driver dropped his coffee thermos bottle from the dash moments before the crash. Police finally opened U.S. Route 209 for traffic at 5:00 p.m., about seven hours after the accident. In the next few days, hundreds of spectators stopped to view the grim scene of the crash.

17

THE GIBBSVILLE CLUB

OCTOBER 15, 1974

Novelist John O'Hara, a native of Pottsville, Pennsylvania, renamed his hometown Gibbsville in his novels. Mahantongo Street—or Lantenego Street as O'Hara dubbed it—was known for wealth and social position. The swanky Gibbsville Club was located on Lantenego Street. In reality, while it was certainly associated with a degree of status in the community, the Pottsville Club was located at 314 Mahantongo Street and opened officially on November 16, 1910.

In 1974, the Pottsville Club was the scene of two nighttime burglaries: one in May and the other in August. Based on the nature of those burglaries, the Pottsville Police Department, while not specifically citing an inside job, indicated that the burglars certainly knew the layout of the building and had key access to an area within the building in at least one of the burglaries. Items stolen included a television, cigarettes, liquor and a relatively small amount of cash.

Early on the morning of October 15, 1974, Pottsville Police patrolman Ronald Gontarchick was on foot patrol at the intersection of Centre and Markets Streets when he was flagged down by a civilian. The man identified himself as the manager of the Pottsville Club. He told Patrolman Gontarchik that he had been struck on the back of the head with a gun carried by assailants who entered the club without his knowledge. He said that he was knocked unconscious. When he awoke, he said he saw smoke from behind the bar. Removing himself from the premises, he made his way downtown to summon help.

The Pottsville Club—or "Gibbsville Club"—as it generally looked during John O'Hara's time in Pottsville. *Schuylkill County Historical Society.*

Gontarchik immediately summoned Sergeant Robert Dusel, who was on patrol in the Fifth Ward, via radio. When informed of the situation, Dusel asked, "Is there anything showing?" Gontarchick replied that he was on the way to the hospital, but with the fog that morning, it was hard to tell if there was a fire in the vicinity. Dusel replied that he was on his way to the area.

Dusel raced to the Pottsville Club. As soon as he arrived, he found smoke pouring from the stately building. He immediately radioed city hall.

"I have a fire at the Pottsville Club. Put the box on!"

The dispatcher came back with, "Which one?"

Dusel spotted fire alarm telegraph Box 36 on the utility pole at Third and Mahantongo Streets.

"Never mind, I'll pull the box myself."

The Gamewell Fire Alarm Telegraph system had been in service in Pottsville since 1890. Specific street corners in Pottsville either featured an actual fire alarm telegraph pull station (i.e., fire alarm box) or had a box number assigned that would direct responding companies to that intersection (i.e. phantom box). The dispatcher on the desk at city hall could transmit the box by placing a brass code wheel with a specific number of teeth that corresponded to the box number assigned to an intersection on the telegraph transmitter. The series of electrical impulses would cause the tape punch register and the house gong in the eight city firehouses to announce the box being received. Firefighters and their apparatus would then race to the street corner that corresponded to that box number.

With that, house gongs and tape punch registers came alive in city firehouses announcing the box alarm from Box 36. The wail of house sirens pierced the early morning air. With a cough of exhaust and a quick rumble, the gasoline motors of fire apparatus came to life in seven of the eight engine rooms of Pottsville fire companies. At a uniquely inopportune time, the Phoenix Fire Company's 1959 American LaFrance 900 Series one-hundred-foot tractor-drawn aerial ladder truck was out of service due to a mechanical issue.

Pottsville's other aerial ladder truck, West End Hose Company's 1960 Seagrave sixty-five-foot 750-GPM quint, was on the way. Swinging left to head east on Mahantongo Street, driver/operator Jerry Coulson danced through the gears as the big Seagrave V-12 motor wound out. While the fog may have masked the smoke somewhat, the scent told the tale blocks away. With the red warning lights reflecting eerily in the fog and smoke, Coulson downshifted as he slowed to enter the block and position the versatile rig in front of the building. He knew that he would have his hands full that morning as he prepared to place both the apparatus pump and aerial ladder in service.

Firefighters were confronted with heavy smoke pushing from the sizeable three-story building of ordinary (i.e. brick and wood) construction. As smaller diameter booster lines and one-and-a-half-inch hose lines were stretched into the main entrance, crews faced a large body of fire near the bar area. Firefighters were taking a beating crawling low under the smoke to close with the flames. Those with the heavy steel cylinders on their backs that were the hallmark of the self-contained breathing apparatus of the era were breathing easily in the smoke. Those old-school, leather-lunged firefighters who eschewed those cumbersome devices drove their chins into their chest as they used helmets, some turned backward, to shield their faces from the heat. The smoke, however, took its toll through squinted, watering eyes and streams of mucous from noses. Crews soon realized that the fire had extended to other areas of the building. Conditions continued to deteriorate, necessitating Fire Chief Andy Hoke withdraw the members from the interior of the property.

Exterior hose streams were driven into the building. Firefighters ascended to the roofs of the exposed properties to attempt to ventilate and operate hose lines. Fire Chief Hoke recognized the absence of the Phoenix aerial ladder truck and the need for an additional aerial device. He requested that the Rescue Hook & Ladder Fire Company from nearby Minersville respond with the company's 1959 C Model Ford/American sixty-five-foot Snorkel. The Minersville Snorkel set up in the rear of the Pottsville Club—directly behind the American Hose Company quarters on West Norwegian Street—and operated effectively by providing an elevated master stream as flames erupted from the upper floors and roof of the building.

As the sun came up that fall morning, smoke and steam hung heavy in the downtown area. Hose streams continued to pour water into the now-gutted Pottsville Club as water runoff poured from the steps leading from the front entrance. Thanks to the tireless work of firefighters, fire damage was limited to the club itself, with the adjoining properties suffering only light smoke and some water damage.

Smoke continues to pour from the top floor and roof of the Pottsville Club after daybreak. Along with the West End Hose Company aerial ladder truck, the Good Will and Good Intent fire companies operated on Mahantongo Street. *Glore collection.*

After a two-and-a-half-hour battle, the fire was placed under control. Fire companies began leaving the scene around ten o'clock that morning. The 150 or so weary firefighters who operated on scene that morning now faced another battle: the clean-up. Hundreds of feet of wet and dirty hose needed to be retrieved and transported back to the firehouse for cleaning and drying. Fresh hose would need to be re-packed on the fire apparatus to ensure emergency readiness. Pottsville firefighters returned to the scene at 2:45 p.m. that day for a flare-up. This fire was quickly quelled. The heavy odor of smoke and wet plaster permeated the downtown area for several days. Damage totaled $325,000.

As the firefighting operations wrapped up, the investigation began in earnest. The tale of assault and burglary was immediately suspect.

While the club manager was under sedation when initially questioned, Police Chief Harold Butts again questioned him when he was more lucid. While he said the story remained basically unchanged, some discrepancies emerged. In addition, the description of the assailants and purported arsonists bordered on the comical:

"What color were his pants?"

"Red."

"What color was his shirt?"

"Red."

"What color were his shoes?"

"Red."

"Was he wearing a hat?"

"Yes."

"What color was the hat?"

"Red."

One Pottsville police officer asked wryly, "Who the hell robbed him, Captain Kangaroo!?"

The other suspect was said to be wearing an army field jacket.

After helping the bandits by opening the safe at gunpoint, the club manager said he had seen one of his assailants start the fire. He later revised his story to indicate that he had seen the assailant *attempt* to start a fire. It was then that he said that he was struck on the back of the head with a handgun and had blacked-out.

In any event, while the cause of the fire was believed to have been incendiary in nature, no charges were brought in the case. The once-handsome "Gibbsville Club" was no more.

18

A CHRISTMAS SEASON NEVER FORGOTTEN

DECEMBER 20, 1980

The 1980 Christmas season was in full swing in McAdoo Borough, and virtually every building and every home in the northeastern Schuylkill County community was gaily decorated for this occasion. Even the town's fire trucks were adorned with holiday decorations as everyone awaited the arrival of Santa Claus, less than five days away. However, this Christmas season would be long remembered for a more somber event: a disastrous fire that struck McAdoo's Business District in the bitter cold morning of December 20, 1980. This blaze threatened to consume an entire block and destroyed a business and an apartment building, leaving three families homeless and without possessions for the Christmas season.

McAdoo police officers first answered a frantic telephone call from an apartment resident of 118 West Blaine Street alerting them of the fire and, while en route to the scene, turned in the fire alarm at 6:11 a.m. The McAdoo Fire Company No. 1 and the Keystone Fire Company of McAdoo soon responded with their trucks and manpower. Police officers at the fire location then roused and evacuated all residents of 118 West Blaine Street and other nearby families as well. The West Blaine Street address housed a large, two-story brick building that included a business, Cara's Bar, and several apartments. Arriving firefighters were immediately confronted with fire completely engulfing Cara's Bar. Additionally, the McAdoo downtown area was totally shrouded in heavy black smoke as the fire continued to gain headway. McAdoo Fire Chief Robert Leshko quickly took command and, realizing the gravity of the situation, placed a call for mutual aid assistance to fire companies in Kelayres, West Hazleton and Hazle Township.

Faced with a raging inferno threatening a sizable downtown area, including several businesses, Chief Leshko placed several large hose lines in operation and ordered the McAdoo ladder truck to position a master water stream in the front of the building in an attempt to dampen the raging fire. Businesses in adjoining buildings threatened by the westward spread of the flames included the Strand Roller Rink, Altasa Blouse Manufacturing Company and several apartments. Also nearby were the McAdoo Post Office and several homes. Chief Leshko ordered the West Hazleton ladder truck, on its quick arrival, into position between the fire building and the adjoining businesses and to operate a master water stream to try to prevent the westward spread of the conflagration. Fortunately, the Strand building was of brick construction and served as a fire wall, inhibiting the flame spread.

With the arrival of the mutual aid companies, over one hundred volunteer firefighters were now battling the blaze in subfreezing temperatures. Any surfaces the hose streams touched soon turned to ice, and ice chunks began falling from power lines and cables in the area.

Flames march through Cara's Bar that bitterly cold day as the McAdoo Fire Company's Seagrave Seventieth Anniversary Series aerial ladder truck operates on scene. *McAdoo Fire Department Collection.*

Owing to the holiday season, the McAdoo Fire Company's FWD pumper is adorned with Christmas decorations as it battles the fire at Cara's Bar. *McAdoo Fire Department Collection.*

Streets and sidewalks were likewise coated in ice, which made footing treacherous. Even worse, firefighters' turnout gear as well as the fire trucks on scene became encased in ice. Such hazardous conditions prompted McAdoo Mayor Joseph C. Billett at 10:00 a.m. to declare a state of emergency in the borough. All streets around the fire scene were cordoned off to traffic and pedestrians by local police and fire police. After several hours of fighting the fire, many firefighters also suffered from exposure to the extreme conditions.

Good Samaritans to the rescue: with the sounding of the municipal fire alarm at 6:11 a.m. and the blaring of sirens from emergency vehicles responding to the scene, sleeping inhabitants of McAdoo were rudely awakened this Saturday morning to the developing tragedy. Soon residents, including entire families, donned overcoats, hats and gloves and converged on the conflagration. Curiosity soon turned to pity as McAdoo residents in this Christmas season soon discovered over one hundred volunteer firefighters, most shrouded in ice, shivering while trying to save buildings, family possessions and the very lives of their residents. Overcome with the desire to aid these heroes, multiple individual residents and entire families went home and delivered an array of sandwiches, hot coffee, hot chocolate,

Christmas cookies and other Coal-Region libations proven to warm the heart and body alike. One McAdoo resident, who remained anonymous, called the local TV station and asked the studio personnel to announce her McAdoo address over the TV, inviting firefighters and other first responders to her living room for a hot meal. Other homes and porches soon became rehab centers for all first responders.

Families and individuals affected by the fire at 118 West Blaine Street were Lois DeBroe and sons Louis and Roy; Glenn Pressler, who lived in a rear apartment; and Dave and June Meron. These residents lost every possession to the fire except the clothes they were wearing when they escaped. Additionally, Helen Lazarus, who lived at 114 West Blaine Street, escaped with her poodle but lost everything else, including her two pet parakeets. Cara's Bar, where the fire was believed to have started, was owned by Frank Cara of Kelayres. This business, too, was destroyed. Adjoining apartments and businesses, including the Strand Roller Rink, Altasa Blouse Manufacturing Company and several additional apartments, while spared from destruction, received smoke and water damage.

After a multi-hour battle under fierce winter conditions, Fire Chief Robert Leshko finally declared the fire under control later Saturday morning. By that time, the destruction caused by this blaze had become readily apparent. McAdoo had lost one of its largest buildings in the business district, and several town families had lost all their possessions. Additionally, a popular bar was also destroyed. Local police and fire police maintained a fire watch throughout the night and into Sunday. McAdoo firefighters were again summoned to the fire scene at 7:00 p.m. for a rekindle when hot embers from the blaze reignited old timber and debris.

State Police Fire Marshal Lawrence Postupack arrived early Monday morning along with local fire and borough officials to investigate the fire scene. While the fire was believed to have started in Cara's Bar, the cause of the fire was never determined due to the widespread destruction that it had caused. In continuing with their Good Samaritan roles, many businesses, including Adam Yakubowski's Store and the American Bank & Trust, conducted clothing and furniture drives, collected monetary donations and held fundraisers to assist the town's victims. Citizens of McAdoo showered praise on McAdoo's firefighters, mutual aid firefighters, local and fire police for their unselfish time and effort and risk of life in controlling this disastrous fire during a Christmas season that will never be forgotten.

19

HORSES AND HORSEPOWER

MARCH 9, 1916

On March 19, 1871, fire destroyed the old town hall building, which was located in the middle of the block on the east side of the 200 block of North Centre Street in downtown Pottsville. Following the fire, a new building was constructed—Centennial Hall. Centennial Hall was three stories in height and was of ordinary (brick and wood) construction. The building came to house the Garden Theater and several stores.

On Thursday night, March 9, 1916, Police Officer John Schnering was walking his beat on Centre Street at approximately 2:00 a.m. Most of the world's attention at that time was on the war raging in Europe. What concerned Schnering at that moment was likely the bitter cold and biting wind—March had indeed come in like a lion. He was walking south on North Centre Street. After crossing the Race Street intersection, he noticed what he thought to be a light left burning in the Garden Theater on the opposite side of the block. He crossed the street to investigate. As he approached the building, he noticed smoke coming from the entrance and hallway of the Garden Theater and also from the south window of the Rouse and Rosenzweig clothing store in the building. He quickly raced the block and a half to the intersection of Center and Market Streets and pulled the hook on fire alarm telegraph Box 18.

House gongs and punch registers came to life in the seven Pottsville firehouses and in city hall—then located in the unit block of North Third Street—as the fire alarm began to bang-in. At this time in Pottsville, the transition had begun from horse-drawn to motorized fire apparatus. Hose and chemical wagons were often the first to respond in this era. A chemical stream was generated through an on-board water tank when a mixture of bicarbonate of soda and sulfuric acid generated carbon dioxide gas within the tank, thereby offering a propellant for the stream of water. Companies began to fire up the internal combustion engines on their hose and chemical wagons and pumpers. Horses were hitched to the remaining steamers and to Phoenix Fire Company's aerial ladder truck. Fire Chief Lynaugh and responding companies could see the column of smoke from throughout the city.

Police officers Miller, Schnering and Madara raced to evacuate residents from the apartment buildings just off the corner of Centre and Arch Streets. They forced the door to one building and removed several families. John Coyle of Philadelphia had been employed in Pottsville for several weeks and was staying in town. Upon hearing the alarm, he helped the police officers in evacuating the neighboring buildings. While in the corner apartment building, he was overcome by smoke and tumbled down a flight of steps, suffering a severe laceration above his eye and bruising about the body.

Firefighters immediately deployed chemical lines and attempted to close with the flames, but conditions deteriorated rapidly. Smoke began to churn from the upper floors as the fire spread. Soon, two-and-a-half-inch hose lines were run from nearby fire hydrants and began to bore into the windows of the building. Realizing that the building was doomed, firefighters focused their efforts on preventing extension to the exposed buildings on either side. In a short time, fire had broken through the roof. With the wind whipping, flying embers began to pose a serious problem.

As the wind was blowing generally from the northwest, the homes along Railroad Street to the rear were immediately threatened. Residents had foreseen the danger and had moved their possessions from the homes. Fairly quickly, fire had taken hold on the roofs of four dwellings to the rear of Centennial Hall. Firefighters repositioned apparatus and hose lines to protect the exposed homes in the rear. Despite their efforts, the homes at 205–11 Railroad Street had the roofs burned off and the top floors gutted. In addition, the roofs of 201 and 203 Railroad Street were destroyed.

At least ten hose lines were stretched, with at least three or four operating in the rear. Water pressure issues were eased when fire department pumpers were placed on the hydrants to pump the handlines. Firefighters also accessed the roofs of the surrounding buildings and used this vantage point to direct several streams. As firefighters struggled to knock down flames in Centennial

The ruins of Centennial Hall in downtown Pottsville continue to smolder following the fire as the front wall has completely collapsed into the street. *Schuylkill County Historical Society.*

Hall and the exposures, flying brands set fire to a few sheds and roofs on the east side of Pottsville, near Greenwood Hill. One flying brand was said to have measured nine and a half inches long and approximately four inches

The rear wall is all that remains standing in this image, which looks from Railroad Street (Progress Avenue today). *Schuylkill County Historical Society.*

thick. Residents of the neighborhood extinguished these fires. The gusting northwest wind was carrying the burning embers some distance.

The night watchman at the Philadelphia and Reading Railroad "Lower Shops"—which generally would have been located on the southeast corner of Route 61 and East Norwegian Street today—discovered smoke in the carpenter shop. He investigated to find that embers had set fire to the wooden framework around the glass skylight. The flames were consuming that portion of the roof area. Fearing that the fire would spread to the stored lumber and oil, he tried desperately to move some lumber. As more and more pieces of burning debris fell on him, he quickly retreated and began to sound the alarm by blowing the shop's steam whistle. When word reached Chief Lynaugh, he quickly sounded a second alarm. Firefighters arriving at the Lower Shops had some difficulty accessing the roof of the building. Adding to their problems were the frozen lines on their chemical engines. Once these two problems were overcome, the fire was quickly extinguished with no additional damage to the shops. This was surely a miraculous feat given the conditions faced and the sheer size of the Lower Shops themselves.

An individual gazes over the icy ruins of the once-proud Centennial Hall building on North Centre Street. *Glore collection.*

Eventually, firefighters began to make headway on the blazing Centennial Hall. The front wall of Centennial Hall began to separate from the building. In an instant, the entire front wall of the building crashed down onto North Centre Street in a huge cloud of smoke and debris. Bricks were scattered everywhere. Firefighters had been positioned well away from the building. There were no injuries reported as a result of the collapse.

The fire was placed under control a little before 7:30 that morning. Fire Chief Lynaugh—having been on the line without a break since the first alarm—arrived at city hall at approximately 7:40 a.m. He said that he literally "hugged" the cast iron radiator in city hall for almost an hour. He later returned to the fireground to begin an origin and cause investigation. Due to the amount of damage, the exact cause of the fire was undetermined; however, it was believed to have been electrical in nature. Chief Lynaugh suspected that the fire originated in the Rouse and Rosenzweg store, as that is where the main body of fire was when he arrived. He also said that it was one of the most difficult fires that he had ever fought.

One firefighter, Lester Wiegand of the Good Intent, suffered a serious fall while fighting the fire. He complained of pain in his left arm all day Thursday. Thursday evening, he went to the doctor. It was discovered that he had a broken wrist.

Companies had returned to quarters throughout the morning after they had sufficiently thawed their frozen equipment to the point that it could be moved. At 11:35 p.m., the fire in Centennial Hall rekindled on what was left of the third floor. Word was quickly sent to city hall. Chief Lynaugh arrived with smoke and sparks flying from the top of the building. A plug stream was deployed and, after some initial difficulty in accessing the location, extinguished this fire. Soon, two other fires were discovered burning in the building. These two were handled with the plug stream. As a precaution, Fire Chief Lynaugh assigned men to a very cold fire watch that night.

Another quite large two-story building was constructed on the site of the Centennial Hall on North Centre Street in Pottsville that served as a bowling alley for many years. As of this writing, it houses the Salvation Army Thrift Store.

20

TEE TIME IS CANCELED!

JULY 26, 1969

O minous black clouds rapidly approached the Fountain Springs Country Club from the west that late Saturday afternoon in July 1969, much to the disappointment of dozens of golfers and club members. As the outside guests scurried for cover, a heavy downpour soon commenced. This Saturday was especially a busy day for the country club, a landmark venue for some of Schuylkill County's and the surrounding areas' most important social events since its opening in 1915. Summer activities were in full swing at the club, and two hundred additional guests were due to arrive shortly for the wedding reception of Mr. and Mrs. James Rhoades, two prominent Mahanoy City residents. This storm, however, soon proved to be an ill omen for the organization.

In its fifty-four years of existence, only four presidents served the Fountain Springs Country Club. Dr. Michael J. Stief of Mount Carmel was the current president and was serving in his eighteenth year at that capacity. Located in Northern Schuylkill County, the country club was considered a premier showplace and had long attracted members from nearby Columbia and Northumberland Counties as well. In addition to the golf course and the golf clubhouse, the country club featured a main clubhouse, a social hall, dining rooms, a bowling alley, a bar and a grille. The large, four-story wood-framed building sat on an idyllic hillside at the base of Broad Mountain, overlooking a vast, lush valley. Its unique architecture and lavish furnishings were hallmarks of the club. The Fountain Springs Country Club served as a setting in several of the novels of John O'Hara, Schuylkill County's most prominent author.

At approximately 6:30 p.m., disaster struck. Amid a torrential downpour, a bolt of lightning walloped the main building with a deafening roar. The lightning strike was heard for several miles in every direction, including the nearby towns of Ashland and Gordon. Dr. Carl Reichwein and Walter Baran, officers of the country club, witnessed the incident and reported that the lightning struck the flagpole attached to the front of the building and "danced" across the roof. Lady golfers in their basement locker room even felt the electric shock. Within minutes of the lightning strike, smoke began to fill the upper floors of the structure. The smoke seemed to emanate from the second-floor apartment of Mr. and Mrs. Ralph Clews, caretakers of the club. Marty Madden Jr., a club employee, grabbed a fire extinguisher and attempted to douse the flames, but the extinguisher failed. Reichwein and Baran soon arrived with extinguishers, and they also attempted to knock down the spreading flames, but their efforts failed as well. While a frantic call was quickly made to the Fountain Springs Fire Company for assistance, Baran and Reichwein evacuated over forty guests from the building without panic.

Fire Chief Edward Helwig soon arrived with Fountain Springs' two Diamond T pumpers and a complement of volunteer members. By the time of their arrival, flames were already engulfing the second floor of the immense

FOUNTAIN SPRINGS COUNTRY CLUB, ASHLAND, PA.

The Fountain Springs Country Club in all its splendor in this picture postcard. *Ashland Historical Society.*

A much different view presented itself to firefighters and onlookers in 1969. The Country Club complex is heavily involved in fire. *Ashland Historical Society.*

wooden structure. A hasty call for assistance was immediately placed to the Ashland Fire Department and other surrounding communities. Ashland Assistant Fire Chief Emerson Hughes responded with the Washington Fire Company's Maxim pumper. Ironically, Ashland Fire Chief John Snyder was hospitalized in nearby Ashland State General Hospital and watched the fire from his hospital bed. The Washington Fire Company laid a hose line from the only fire hydrant near the club, but flames were already consuming the upper floors. News of the fire quickly spread faster than the fire itself, and soon hundreds of spectators in addition to arriving wedding reception guests converged on the scene.

As a teenager at the time, Philip Groody of Ashland remembers the storm and lightning strike very well. Philip described it as "one hell of a storm." Philip reported that the lightning strike was heard throughout the town, and it was soon followed by the sounding of the Ashland fire alarm. Philip's

father, an avid golfer and club member, and Philip drove to the fire scene in his father's new 1969 Chevrolet pickup truck and witnessed the destruction personally. Chaos ensued at the fire scene as Country Club Road was soon snarled by dozens of vehicles, often hindering the responding fire trucks. Hundreds of spectators also gathered at the nearby Ashland State General Hospital and the Ashland Nursing School grounds for a bird's-eye view of the developing disaster. The Citizens' Fire Company of Gordon soon arrived with their two Chevrolet pumpers along with the Friendship Fire Company of Englewood with their Hahn fire truck. Frackville's Good Will Fire Company also answered the call and sent its Seagrave fire truck, and the Lavelle Volunteer Fire Company responded with its FWD pumper.

Close to one hundred volunteer firefighters battled the flames for three hours, but with a limited water supply from the only nearby fire hydrant, their efforts to save the country club were in vain. Assistant Fire Chief Emerson Hughes stated that the blaze was far out of control, and flames were shooting through the roof when we arrived. Hughes stated, "It was gone when we got there." Firefighters then directed their efforts toward saving the nearby golf clubhouse, which was separated from the main building by an eighteen-inch fire wall. Through their efforts, the golf clubhouse was spared destruction but received considerable water damage. The advancing

Evening Herald.

SHENANDOAH – ASHLAND – MAHANOY CITY

GOOD EVENING

MONDAY, JULY 28, 1969

SINGLE COPY: 10c

$300,000 Loss as Fire Destroys Country Club

FIRE WRECKS LANDMARK — Evening Herald photographer Bob Kyler of Ashland catches the furious fire at its height Saturday afternoon at Fountain Springs Country Club. Firemen at right are standing on the roof of the locker room and grille, which they saved from fire damage. However, the locker area was soaked with water. Bottom photo shows the bleak scene on Sunday, with only the two chimneys remaining where the 34-year-old showplace stood. The structure was leveled in 20 minutes.

Nixon in Thailand

Bloodmobile Due Tuesday

Mahanoy City Fire Hits Vacant Homes

8th Michigan Coed Slain

Nine GIs Are Killed As VC Hits Copter

Freak Twister Hits Zion Grove Vicinity

Frackville Man, 85, Missing on Mountain

Above: The *Evening Herald* newspaper of Shenandoah announces the destruction of the Fountain Springs County Club.

Opposite: The scope of the blaze is readily evident as viewed from a distance. *Ashland Historical Society.*

flames, however, soon completely engulfed and quickly consumed the main clubhouse building.

Three hours after the lightning strike, the Fountain Springs Country Club was leveled with only its foundations and two large chimneys remaining. The only object reportedly saved from the building was the organization's charter. Dr. Carl Reichwein of Ashland was the last person to leave the building, losing his eyeglasses in the process. Two Ashland firefighters, Fred Shilling and Joseph Cuthie, were both treated for minor burns in the Ashland Community Ambulance, which had also responded to the scene. One Ashland firefighter, Edward Hughes, was treated at the scene for smoke inhalation. Damage estimates by club officers ranged between $300,000 and $350,000, with only part of that loss covered by insurance. That very evening, Dr. Michael J. Stief, club president, while standing in front of the smoldering embers of his club, immediately pledged that the Fountain Springs Country Club would rise again. Stief and other club officers thanked the volunteer firefighters for their valiant efforts that summer evening.

On March 4, 1971, almost twenty months after the disastrous fire, members of the press and media were invited by President Michael J. Stief to a dinner and a tour of the new Fountain Springs Country Club facility. Members and guests attended an official dedication and grand opening on March 28, 1971. In newspaper ads throughout the region, the Fountain Springs Country Club thanked the general public for their patience and strong support in the club's rebuilding efforts. Thus, a new chapter in the long history of the Fountain Springs Country Club commenced.

On an interesting side note, the country club fire was Ashland Fire Chief John Snyder's last fire that he witnessed in his long, distinguished career. Chief Snyder succumbed to his health issues at the Ashland State General Hospital the following week. Philip Groody, who, as a teenager, heard the lightning strike and witnessed the destruction firsthand, soon began his long-term and prominent role with the Ashland Fire Department, serving for decades as fire chief. Dr. Carl Reichwein attended the medical needs of Ashland's residents for almost fifty years. Walter Baran became a Pennsylvania cabinet member under Governor Richard Thornburgh, and James Rhoades, whose wedding reception was abruptly ended by the fire, became a Pennsylvania state senator. His wife, Mary Edith Rhoades, was this author Michael Kitsock's favorite Mahanoy Area High School English teacher!

21

ONE DRINK TOO MANY

JANUARY 2, 1911

The temperance movement, established for the prohibition of all alcohol usage, gained considerable power and support both locally, statewide and throughout the United States in the early twentieth century. Temperance societies likewise sprang up in communities in all areas of Schuylkill County during this time. Deadly disasters caused by alcohol abuse, such as this Minersville incident, sparked the drive to banish all alcohol usage, resulting in the passing of the Eighteenth Amendment to the United States Constitution on January 16, 1919. And the incident begins:

On New Year's Day, Sunday, January 1, 1911, a celebration was held at the Kosalavage house on Sunbury Street, between Fourth and Fifth Streets in Minersville. This house also served as a boardinghouse for foreigners, mostly miners. It was reported that after celebrating throughout the day, several "foreigners" congregated at the home for a "last call." This gathering began to break up after midnight on Monday, January 2. One of the revelers, who had imbibed a great deal of alcohol, returned to his room about 2:00 a.m. He inadvertently knocked over an oil lamp, which quickly set fire to nearby combustible materials. This man fled his room and the building, but no immediate alarm of fire was sounded.

Dr. Monahan, whose home and office were directly across the street from the Kosalavage dwelling, arose to some commotion outside and noticed smoke issuing from the building. The alarm was then transmitted. Minersville's telegraph alarm system had been installed in 1910. Dr. Monahan ran across the street and kicked in the door and escorted Mr. and

A vintage postcard gives the viewer a look at the borough of Minersville as it generally existed at the time of the 1911 fire. The Kosalavage home would have stood in the center-right of the photo in the 400 block of Sunbury Street. *Today in Minersville Collection.*

Mrs. Kosalavage, both only partially clad, from the building. Dr. Monahan immediately asked the Kosalavages if their children had been removed from the building. He was assured that they were safe. Residents were evacuated from the adjoining buildings as well. All awaited the arrival of the four Minersville's fire companies: Mountaineer, Independent, Good Will and Rescue Hook & Ladder. At that time, Mountaineer was operating a hose carriage and an 1866 Amoskeag third-size steam pumper. Independent was equipped with a four-wheel hose carriage. Good Will arrived with an 1897 Muskegan chemical wagon. Rescue was operating an 1875 hand-drawn rig, which may have been an early chemical wagon.

The companies arrived with smoke beginning to push from the rooming house and the neighboring dwellings. Firefighters were repeatedly assured that all occupants had escaped the fire. Chemical lines were immediately deployed as two-and-a-half-inch lines were stretched from nearby hydrants. The fire, however, began to take possession of the Kosalavage home and extend to the adjacent homes.

Suddenly the father of the children began to shriek wildly and ran back into the house. His wife collapsed where she was. Firefighters quickly removed Mr. Kosalavage , but not before he was seriously burned on the face and hands. As flames began to pour from the windows of the home, firefighters and onlookers began to realize the tragedy that was now taking shape. The Kosalavages had recovered enough from their drunken stupor to realize that their children were still in the now heavily involved building.

Firefighters placed ladders to the involved home and drove hose streams into the flames. In addition to their efforts to knock down the flames in the Kosalavage home, firefighters also battled flames now raging in the adjoining homes. While three homes were gutted, firefighters managed to prevent the flames from damaging the other neighboring buildings. After several hours, firefighters had the main body of fire knocked down. Conditions were such that they were able to enter the Kosalavage dwelling. Reluctantly they began the task that all firefighters dread: they searched the home for the children. In short order, the scope of the tragedy would soon be known. The five

The Mountaineer Hose Company of Minersville is shown in parade form on Sunbury Street in Minersville circa 1950 with the company's 1866 Amoskeag third-size steam fire engine, which was purchased from the Good Intent Fire Company of Pottsville. The "Mounties" steamer would have responded to the tragic Kosalavage fire in 1911, also on Sunbury Street. *Glore collection.*

Kosalavage children, three boys and two girls, had perished in the fire. The children ranged in age from two months to eight years.

Firefighters, bystanders and especially Dr. Monahan were devastated. All were convinced that had they been aware that the children had not yet escaped the home, they could have been rescued early in the fire. By the time it was discovered that the children were still inside the home, it was too late. Mr. and Mrs. Kosalavage were removed to Pottsville Hospital for treatment.

The five children were buried at the Saint Francis of Assisi Lithuanian Cemetery on Friday, January 5. Five hundred people joined in the procession from Saint Francis of Assisi Lithuanian Catholic Church on Third Street to the cemetery following a funeral Mass.

The parents of the children were largely condemned following the fire and the funeral for, first, their evident lack of concern for the safety and welfare of their children and, second, for the level of intoxication of the adults in the home at the time of the fire. The local newspaper, however, had a different view on the second charge. The newspaper took a direct aim at the American public and the encouragement it gave to "drunken revelry." It also cited law enforcement for its lax enforcement of the existing liquor laws. Prohibition was still eight years away, but the temperance movement had taken a firm hold by this time. Based on a preliminary review, it appears that this was the deadliest fire in Minersville's history.

GLOSSARY

accelerant Some substance, usually a flammable liquid, that is used to increase the spread of fire.

aerial ladder truck Firefighting apparatus equipped with a heavy-duty extension ladder affixed to the truck itself, which is used for rescue from height, to provide access to the upper stories or roofs of buildings or to provide an elevated master stream.

apparatus Generally, the equipment and machinery needed, assembled and deployed for a particular purpose. In this case, fire apparatus consists of vehicles specifically designed to combat fires or provide special equipment necessary to rescue those trapped by fire or other means.

arson The criminal act of deliberately setting fire to property.

backdraft An explosion that occurs when oxygen is suddenly introduced to accumulated gases that are byproducts of incomplete combustion.

booster line The booster system replaced the chemical tank (see next page) circa 1913. With a booster system, an apparatus pump was used to generate pressure to propel the water in the on-board tank through a hose line. This hose line—like the chemical line it replaced—was a hard rubber hose generally of three-quarters of an inch or an inch in diameter.

box alarm A response assignment of fire apparatus designated for a specific geographic area that corresponds to a numeric designation. Largely originating with the streetcorner telegraph fire alarm boxes, the box number (e.g., 41) would call for a number and type of fire companies to respond to that location, usually the closest. Today the process is largely computerized but follows the same general concept. In most instances, a box alarm is transmitted for a structural fire response.

bunker gear Fire-resistant clothing ensemble to protect the firefighter in the course of his or her duties. This would include boots, pants, coat, protective hood, gloves and helmet.

chemical engine/chemical wagon Deployed from the latter half of the nineteenth century through the early decades of the twentieth century, a chemical system consisted of a tank of water in which was mixed a solution of bicarbonate of soda. Into this was introduced a vial of sulfuric acid (oil of vitriol). This mixture generated a significant amount of carbon dioxide (carbonic acid) gas. This pressure then immediately propelled a stream of water from the tank through a hard rubber hose and onto the flames. These systems were installed on a wide variety of fire apparatus pulled by hand, horse-drawn or motorized. Water capacity of the chemical tanks was generally thirty-five to forty gallons.

cockloft The area of a structure that occupies the space between the underside of the roof deck and the top floor ceiling. In row homes in some instances, this space may be open across the entire row.

engine/pumper Firefighting apparatus equipped with a fire pump designed to supply water from an onboard tank, a positive source (i.e., a fire hydrant) or a static source (i.e., a pond). the pump would then build pressure to supply the water through firefighting hose streams.

exposure A building or place considered to be potentially threatened by flames. This could be a building next to, in front of or behind a building that is on fire.

flashover That stage of fire development in which a room or other given space becomes heated to the point that flames envelope the entire space with extreme rapidity.

gallons per minute (GPM) The rated capacity of a pump mounted on fire apparatus.

hydraulic rescue tools (HRT)/"jaws of life" The family of rescue tools that uses hydraulic pressure to power tools designed to push, pull, cut and spread. While there are many applications, these tools are commonly used to rescue passengers trapped in motor vehicle accidents.

incendiary fire A fire that is intentionally ignited in an area and under circumstances in which there should be no fire.

ladder pipe A nozzle affixed to the end of an aerial ladder capable of providing a large-caliber water stream from height.

mask/all-purpose mask Prior to the widespread use of SCBA (see next page) this device featured a filtering container usually worn at the firefighter's chest, which cleaned particulate contaminants from smoke, supplying somewhat "cleaner" air through a tightly fitting face mask. It did not, however, remove all toxic gases, nor did it supply clean breathing air. this device is commonly referred to as a gas mask.

master stream A heavy-caliber water stream that can be played from a fixed monitor on a fire apparatus or supplied by one or more hose lines and operated from a more portable device.

nozzle The controlling device on the end of a hose line. The water flow is typically controlled by a handle that manipulates a built-in valve.

ordinary construction A type of building construction that is characterized by noncombustible exterior walls (i.e., brick, masonry) and combustible (i.e., wood) floors, roofs and interior walls.

primary search A rapid search of a fire building for potential victims that is typically conducted prior to the fire having been controlled.

quad A firefighting apparatus that combines four essential functions: a fire pump, a water tank and a hose complement, as well as a full complement of portable ground ladders.

quint A firefighting apparatus that combines five essential functions: a fire pump, a water tank, a hose complement, a full complement of ground ladders, as well as an aerial ladder device.

row home/row house One of a series of homes that are connected by common sidewalls. These homes then form a continuous group, often extended an entire block. These homes are typically of wood frame or ordinary construction.

secondary search As opposed to the primary search, a secondary search typically occurs after the fire has been placed under control. This search is more deliberate and thorough.

self-contained breathing apparatus (SCBA) A cylinder containing breathing air and ancillary equipment that allows a firefighter to breathe clean air through a mask tightly sealed around the face.

snorkel While referencing a specific company that largely pioneered the devices, the term *snorkel* has come to generally define an articulating boom on which is affixed a platform or "bucket" from which firefighters can affect rescues or delivery a heavy-caliber water stream from an elevated position with a relative degree of safety and stability.

turnout gear/running gear As opposed to bunker gear, this firefighting ensemble typically featured a longer coat, hip boots, helmet and, in the latter part of the twentieth century, gloves.

ventilation Essentially, the process of removing heat, smoke and fire gases from within a burning building to allow the advance of a hose line to extinguish the flames and to allow for more rapid advance of the primary search. in coordination with fire extinguishment, ventilation improves conditions for firefighters and civilians alike. This is typically exemplified by breaking window glass or cutting holes in the roof.

wood frame A type of building construction in which primary structural components—exterior and interior walls, roofs and floors—are made entirely or partially of wood.

ABOUT THE AUTHORS

Michael R. Glore and Michael J. Kitsock are veteran firefighters and have coauthored three previous books: *Pottsville Firefighting*, *Schuylkill County Firefighting* and *Reading Firefighting*. Glore served as assistant fire chief of Pottsville, Pennsylvania, from 2004 to 2007. In 2007, Glore became a career firefighter with the City of Reading, Pennsylvania, and, since 2022, he has served as first deputy chief of the Reading Fire Department. Kitsock is a fifty-year veteran in the volunteer fire service and an instructor emeritus for the Pennsylvania State Fire Academy. Kitsock also serves as an assistant fire chief in Norwegian Township, Pennsylvania. Both authors share a strong passion for the rich history of the fire service in their home county.

Visit us at
www.historypress.com